T0334079

Cambridge Elements ≡

Elements in Metaphysics
edited by
Tuomas E. Tahko
University of Bristol

METAPHYSICAL REALISM
AND ANTI-REALISM

JTM Miller
Durham University

CAMBRIDGE
UNIVERSITY PRESS

CAMBRIDGE
UNIVERSITY PRESS

University Printing House, Cambridge CB2 8BS, United Kingdom

One Liberty Plaza, 20th Floor, New York, NY 10006, USA

477 Williamstown Road, Port Melbourne, VIC 3207, Australia

314–321, 3rd Floor, Plot 3, Splendor Forum, Jasola District Centre,
New Delhi – 110025, India

103 Penang Road, #05–06/07, Visioncrest Commercial, Singapore 238467

Cambridge University Press is part of the University of Cambridge.

It furthers the University's mission by disseminating knowledge in the pursuit of
education, learning, and research at the highest international levels of excellence.

www.cambridge.org
Information on this title: www.cambridge.org/9781009009089
DOI: 10.1017/9781009006927

© JTM Miller 2022

First published 2022

A catalogue record for this publication is available from the British Library.

ISBN 978-1-009-00908-9 Paperback
ISSN 2633-9862 (online)
ISSN 2633-9854 (print)

Metaphysical Realism and Anti-Realism

Elements in Metaphysics

DOI: 10.1017/9781009006927
First published online: June 2022

JTM Miller
Durham University

Author for correspondence: JTM Miller, james.miller@durham.ac.uk

Abstract: Minimally, metaphysical realists hold that there exist some mind-independent entities. Metaphysical realists also (tend to) hold that we can speak meaningfully or truthfully about mind-independent entities. Those who reject metaphysical realism deny one or more of these commitments. This Element aims to introduce the reader to the core commitments of metaphysical realism and to illustrate how these commitments have changed over time by surveying some of the main families of views that realism has been contrasted with, such as (radical) scepticism, idealism, and anti-realism.

Keywords: metaphysical realism, metaphysical anti-realism, existence, mind-independence, accessibility

ISBNs: 9781009009089 (PB), 9781009006927 (OC)
ISSNs: 2633-9862 (online), 2633-9854 (print)

Contents

1 Introduction

The term 'realism' has perhaps inspired more philosophical literature and discussion than any other within the field – the philosophical term that has launched a thousand theories and counter-theories. Almost all, if not actually all, branches of philosophy have produced literature that discusses some view labelled 'realism'. There are debates about semantic realism, moral realism, scientific realism, property realism, realism about universals, and a whole host more.

In each of these cases, realism concerns initially the *existence* of a certain sort of entity (or entities). A moral realist thinks that there are moral properties (or facts). A property realist thinks that there are properties. However, this is insufficient as a characterisation of realism. Most think that it is not enough to think that such entities exist to be a realist about them. We also need to hold that the entities are in some sense independent: that the entities in question need to have features or nature that is distinct from how we happen to think or talk about those entities. An aesthetic realist, for example, does not simply think that beauty exists, but additionally thinks that facts about whether something is beautiful exist independently of how we happen to think or talk. The relevant properties or facts are '*mind-independent*'.

This Element, though, is not about any of those forms of realism, nor is it about realism in general. It is about 'metaphysical realism'. So what is metaphysical realism? Metaphysical realism concerns the entities posited by metaphysics. Given that metaphysics is typically taken by its practitioners at least to be about 'everything', 'reality', or 'the world', metaphysical realism is, on the first pass, the view that the world exists and is mind-independent. Or, in slightly less grandiose terms, that there are *things* – entities of some sort – that exist and are the way that they are independent of how we happen to talk or think about them. Where other forms of realism argue in favour of the existence and independence of one sort of entity – for example, moral realism holds that moral properties or facts exist – metaphysical realism is more general in scope. Metaphysical realists might (and do) disagree about *what* exists but agree that some *thing* does and that those existents, whatever they are, are 'mind-independent'.

As we will see throughout this Element, this first pass take on metaphysical realism is too crude and needs significant fine-tuning. I will attempt to make it more precise in Section 2. I will distinguish various forms of realism and outline some core commitments of metaphysical realism. Most important are the 'existence', 'independence', and 'accessibility' commitments. I will leave the details for later, but in slogan form, these, in turn, commit the realist to the existence of some entity, the mind-independence of that entity (or the mind-independence of some of its properties), and our ability to know about (or access) such mind-independent entities.

Metaphysical realism, at this point, might sound like a common-sense position. Of course, there are mind-independent entities, some readers will be thinking. The existence of mind-independent entities might feel like an obvious truth, derivable just from your own experience of the world and the things within it. To deny this might seem strange or even contradictory. However, although metaphysical realism is often described (by realists) as the 'default view', there have been too many objections and anti-realist views developed to be able to mention them all in an Element like this.

Furthermore, the objections have changed over time. Someone that rejects metaphysical realism today will have different reasons and alternative views than someone rejecting metaphysical realism a few hundred years ago. My aim for this Element is to be a guide to how metaphysical realism is understood *now*, but understanding what it means to be a metaphysical realist *now* requires some understanding of how the notion of metaphysical realism has changed over time, often due to the need to respond to certain anti-realist arguments or positions.

Given this, in Section 3, I will focus on outlining some of the most prominent and influential rejections of metaphysical realism in (roughly) chronological order. By looking at the objections to metaphysical realism in this way, we will be able to see how with each new objection, or form of anti-realism, the realist has taken on additional commitments. Metaphysical realism thus begins as the default view. And it is only as objections are raised that the realist's commitments are made explicit. My hope is that examining the alternatives to metaphysical realism in this way will help illuminate the nature of metaphysical realism itself

In Section 4, I will discuss the prospects for defending metaphysical realism more broadly. This is (by some distance) the shortest section of the Element. This is not because I think that there are no good reasons to be a metaphysical realist. Indeed, I am myself a metaphysical realist (though I tend to think that there is more right about some anti-realist arguments than many other metaphysical realists). Rather, the shortness of this section merely reflects that metaphysical realists somewhat rarely directly argue *for* metaphysical realism, but instead argue *against* anti-realism. This, combined with the common defence of metaphysical realism as the default view (see Section 2.5), has a consequence that the realism debate can often feel like a stalemate. In Section 4, I will allow myself some (hopefully not too wild) speculations about the future of the realism debate and some speculation about how we might in the future avoid this stalemate.

What it means to be a metaphysical realist will certainly change in the future. The ever-changing nature of the realism/anti-realism debate is, in my view, part of the reason why it has continued to be important to generations of philosophers. The sections and subsections of this Element are intended to be (relatively) readable in isolation. Thus, if the reader's interest is in one aspect of metaphysical realism, or the rejection of one particularly core commitment of realism, my hope is the relevant sections can be read independently of each other without too much loss of understanding, and help those new to the debate find their feet within it.

Before we begin, there are some important caveats on the intended scope of this Element. As will hopefully become clear, the aim of this Element will not be to provide the single correct account of what it means to be a metaphysical realist or anti-realist. I do not conceive of this Element as being an argument for (or against) a particular definition. Part of the reason for this is that I am somewhat sceptical that there is a correct single definition of metaphysical realism that can be consistently applied throughout the history of philosophy. For example, within the Western philosophical tradition, before around the middle of the twentieth century, the label 'anti-realist' was not used much with respect to questions about metaphysical realism. Metaphysical realism was instead primarily contrasted with idealism. Even in the early twentieth century, the focus was still on the realist–idealist debate. Carnap, one of the major influences on contemporary metaphysical realism-anti-realism debates, for example, aims to dissolve the disagreement between realism and idealism (see Carnap 1963: 17–18). This is not to say that there is no correct account of metaphysical realism. Perhaps there is, but I am not sure myself what it is, and I do not think that we have got to it yet.

Nor will I go into too much detail about the possible consequences of being a metaphysical realist, anti-realist, or idealist. Being able to label an opposing view as 'realist' (or 'anti-realist') has been taken to have various consequences, and what those consequences are has also shifted throughout history. For example (and with thanks to David Edmunds' superb historical account of the Vienna Circle), the realist–idealist debate had significant political significance in the early twentieth century, with the realism debate being invoked by Lenin as part of his power struggles with his rivals. (For those interested, Lenin was on the side of 'realism' (see Marx, Engels, and Lenin 1972), but many Bolsheviks viewed the realist commitment to 'absolute truth' and to the reality of the external world as being 'bourgeois and old-fashioned' (Edmunds 2020: 10).) I will not comment in this Element on these sorts of consequences of being a metaphysical realist or anti-realist. It is certainly an interesting (if understudied) topic. But, due to space limitations, I will keep the discussion in this Element narrowly constrained to certain core metaphysical and ontological issues.

Lastly, it is worth noting that I am not primarily a historian of philosophy, and my training is almost entirely within the Western tradition. My apologies, then, to historians of philosophy and experts in other philosophical traditions for not commenting on many important figures and traditions. By leaving any views or figures out, or only giving them a passing mention, I am not intending to in any way downplay their significance or importance. Rather, because of the short length, wide scope, and introductory aims of this Element, it is not possible to provide a full reconstruction of all the relevant philosophers and philosophies that could be covered in work with a narrower focus. I will do my best to point interested readers to more in-depth discussions, but the topics covered in this Element should not be viewed as being (or trying to be) comprehensive.

2 What Is Metaphysical Realism?

2.1 Distinguishing Realism

Let us begin by distinguishing metaphysical realism from other forms of realism. At its most general, realism concerns the *existence* and *independence* of entities (where I use the term 'entities' as a catch-all general term for any *thing*, be it an object, property, fact, event, substance, process, etc.). For example, Alexander Miller defines *generic* realism as the view that '[Entities] a, b, and c and so on exist, and the fact that they exist and have properties such as F-ness, G-ness, and H-ness is (apart from mundane empirical dependencies of the sort sometimes encountered in everyday life) independent of anyone's beliefs, linguistic practices, conceptual schemes, and so on' (Miller 2019).

This 'generic realism' is intended to provide an account that can then be applied to various more specific, or local, cases. Generic realism, as defined by Miller at least, is more like a template for other forms of realism. Using this template, we can define some local realism about some entity, x, as the view that holds that x exists, and that x exists independently of how we happen to think or talk about x. A local anti-realist about x is then taken to be a denial of either (or both) the existence of x, or the independence of the properties possessed by x from our beliefs, linguistic practices, conceptual schemes, and so on.

Local realism (or anti-realism) is limited in that it is a claim about those specific entities only: if I accept the existence of the Loch Ness Monster, I could be said to be a realist about the Loch Ness Monster as I believe that there is some x such that x is the Loch Ness Monster. This is, by itself, only a form of *local* realism as accepting the existence of Nessie does not commit me to the existence or non-existence of other entities. It says nothing about the existence of tables, moral facts, properties, unobservable entities, propositions, or any other entities, being only a commitment to realism about large loch-dwelling prehistoric creatures. Given the limited scope of local realism and anti-realism, most people are local anti-realists about some entity or entities. Few, if anybody, thinks that *everything* exists and is mind-independent (though some do hold that *nothing* exists or is mind-independent; see Sections 3.1 and 3.2).

Very often, when philosophers use the term 'realism', this is a shorthand for some form of local realism, with (one of) the major differences between the forms of local realism being what sort of entities it is that they are concerned with. Moral realism is a form of local realism committed to the existence of moral properties (or facts); scientific realism is a form of local realism committed to the existence of non-observable entities; aesthetic realism is a form of local realism committed to the existence of (objective) aesthetic properties; realism about properties is a form of local realism committed to the existence of (universal) properties; and so on for various other realisms that we might consider.

Metaphysical realism differs from forms of local realism in its scope. Whereas local realisms concern whether some particular entity or kind of entity exist, metaphysical realism is about whether *any* entity (or entities) exist. Metaphysical realism is realism as applied to 'reality' or 'the world'. Metaphysical realism is therefore often described as being 'global'. Thus, if we use the generic realism template, but apply it to metaphysical realism, we get the result that metaphysical realism is the view that the world exists, and that the world exists independently of how we happen to think or talk about the world.

This is fine as a way of understanding metaphysical realism to begin with, but we need to clarify what we mean by 'the world'. There is a reading 'the world' that would suggest that the metaphysical realist is committed to the existence (and independence) of every *thing*. That is, for every a, b, c,..., n, the metaphysical realist is committed to the existence and independence of a, b, c,..., n.

This, though, would not be accurate. The metaphysical realist need not be a realist with respect to all entities covered by the multitude of local realisms. To be a metaphysical realist does not mean that we necessarily are committed to scientific realism, moral realism, aesthetic realism, and so on. And being a local anti-realist about the Loch Ness Monster would not necessarily mean that we are committed to metaphysical anti-realism. Rather, metaphysical realism is general or global in the sense that the metaphysical realist thinks (minimally, pending later extensions) that at least one entity exists and it is independent of us. A commitment to metaphysical realism does not commit us to the existence of any particular entity or sort of entity – only to there being *some* (suitably mind-independent) entity.

This point should be stressed as the term 'metaphysical realism' has been used for various purposes throughout history, and one not uncommon use is for the term to refer to realist views about this or that particular sort or kind of entity. For example, Bigelow writes that 'the doctrine that there are universals (other than sets) is often called "metaphysical realism" or "realism about universals"' (Bigelow 2010: 472). So understood, metaphysical realism is specifically a position about the existence and mind-independence of universal properties (as opposed to 'nominalists' that reject the existence of such entities). This use of 'metaphysical realism' is not uncommon, but could cause confusion here.

Metaphysical realism, as I wish to understand it here, is a broader claim than a form of realism concerned with the existence (and mind-independence) of one particular sort of entity. It is realism as applied to the world. Accepting realism about universal properties therefore entails accepting metaphysical realism as it is to be understood here. If we accept that universal properties exist, then we are accepting that there is at least one entity that exists and is mind-independent. But the converse does not hold. We can be metaphysical realists, as I intend the term, without being realists about universal properties. So long as the nominalist about properties thinks that (at least some) of the particular properties they posit are mind-independent, they too will be metaphysical realists, even though they reject the existence of *universal* properties.

Putting this another way, as it will be discussed here, metaphysical realism is a view that does not concern itself with *what* exists. Rather, it is a view about *whether* some thing exists, and whether those things that exist are mind-independent. One metaphysical realist could hold that realist contains only one (or one sort of) mind-independent entity; another could hold that there are multiple entities (or multiple sorts of entities). So long as both hold that those entities exist and are mind-independent, both would be forms of metaphysical realism for our purposes here. This is not to deny that there are interesting debates to be had concerning the existence and mind-independence of universal properties (and properties more broadly). It is only to say that that debate is not the focus here. Other books in this Elements series will cover those topics and the relevant more specific forms of realism and anti-realism.

This, hopefully, provides a start towards a clearer sense what it means to be a metaphysical realist, but terms like 'existence' and 'mind-independence', need much further analysis, and we need to consider various other additional commitments that metaphysical realists typically accept. It is to these that I now turn. From now on though, we can at least simplify things a little bit: having distinguished metaphysical realism from other forms of realism, from now on, unless otherwise specified, we can drop the term 'metaphysical' and simply talk of 'realism'.

2.2 Two Core Commitments of Metaphysical Realism

2.2.1 Existence

The first and seemingly most straight forward of the commitments is to the existence of (at least one) entity. As already noted, *what* exists is not strictly important for the sort of realism under discussion here. All that the realist is committed to is that there is some *thing*. The existent might be any sort or kind of entity, although, as we will see, some additional restrictions do emerge when the existence commitment is combined with the independence commitment.

It is important to note that by accepting existence, the realist is *not* taking any position on what it is for something to exist. That is, realists can agree that something exists but disagree about what criterion an entity must fulfil to exist. Realists might therefore understand ontological commitment in any of the ways put forward in the literature on that topic (see Parent 2020), just so long as they think that there is some entity that does fulfil that requirement.

Existence is clearly a very minimal commitment. If this commitment exhausted what it is to be a realist, the requirements for realism would, for most, be easily satisfied, and it would leave very few options available to oppose realism (though there would be some; see Section 3.1). Given this, while it is a necessary condition for a view to be classified as realist, it is not viewed as a sufficient condition.

2.2.2 (Mind-)Independence

Devitt, recognising the limitations in the existence criterion as the sole commit- ment of realism, characterises realism as being the combination of two claims. The first is the above existence claim – simply that to be a realist is to be committed to the existence of some *thing* or *things*. On the second, Devitt writes: 'words that frequently occur in attempts to capture the second are "independent", "external" and "objective". The entities must be independent of the mental; they must be external to the mind; they must exist objectively in that they exist whatever anyone's opinions' (Devitt 1983: 292). Devitt is therefore a realist because he thinks that 'common sense, and scientific, physical entities objectively exist independent of the mental' (Devitt 1983: 292). To be a realist, for Devitt, is to accept 'something so apparently humdrum as the independent existence of the familiar world' (Devitt 1991: vii).

What this often amounts to is a claim that realism requires us to think that there are *mind-independent* entities such that that mind-independence is part of their nature. It is not enough to think that there exists some *thing* to be realist. Rather, to be a realist, there must exist some entity, *and* the nature of that entity – the way that it is – is independent of how we happen to think, talk, or perceive it. Thus, the existence of such entities, and the ways that those entities are, are objective or independent of us. This is (partly) why the debate around realism is often phrased in terms of properties, as properties are taken to determine the nature or way that some entity is. Put in these terms, the realist thinks that there are some objects that have (at least some of) their properties mind-independently. The anti-realist will deny this.

However, although this characterisation might seem innocuous at first, the difficulty comes in clarifying what exactly we mean by 'independent', 'mind-independent', 'external', or 'objective'. Each of these could be cashed out in various ways and in ways that do (or do not) make them synonyms. Potentially adding to the confusion, several realists have employed various metaphorical notions to try to help illuminate this matter, perhaps most famously that of the 'God's-Eye view on the world'. To reject realism is to reject that there is some '"God's-Eye" point of view, from which we could compare our theories and belief about the world to the world itself, as it is independently of our conceptual systems' (Haukioja 2020: 67). These metaphors, though, are unlikely to be satisfying to those predisposed to be suspicious of realism.

Unsurprisingly, then, there has been a significant amount of literature that attempts to capture more precisely what we might mean by '(mind)-independence', 'external', and 'objective', and whether these terms are synonyms after all. The rest of this section aims to clarify some of the disagreements over these notions and work towards some clearer sense of what the realist is committed to when they accept that there are 'mind-independent' entities.

A first complication is that there are ways of understanding mind-independence such that many objects that we interact with become mind-dependent entities. The computer that I am working at, for example, might be thought to be a mind-dependent object, as were it not for the actions of minds that design and create computers, my computer would not exist. The same goes for the mug on my desk, the desk itself, and even the tea that I am drinking. After all, we might think that without the mental states of various people, the tea I am drinking would not have been grown, processed, and available for me to buy in the supermarket.

And yet, there is a clear sense in which such mind-dependence claims are 'mundane' (Jenkins 2005: 199). Accepting that the artefacts around us are in some sense mind-dependent does not force us to reject realism immediately. What the realist means by mind-independence is that despite the role that minds play in the creation of various entities, there is still something about those entities – some aspect of their nature – that is mind-independent. Even though minds may have been involved in the creation of some entity, now that it does exist, both some aspect of that entity's nature and its continued existence are not dependent on my mind (or indeed any mind even those with far greater cognitive power than we have as humans). What this means is that whatever entities a realist posits, the realist need not think that *every* entity is mind-independent, only that some are. Nor that every aspect (or property) of the entity is mind-independent. My computer might be mind-dependent in the way outlined above, but a realist might hold that it is mind-independent as some of its properties (its shape and weight, for example) are had by the computer irrespective of how I talk, think, or perceive the computer.

This does introduce the question of *which* entities, or which properties of entities, are mind-independent and how might we be able to distinguish between those that are mind-dependent and those that are mind-independent. Perhaps my computer is entirely mind-dependent. Perhaps the only mind-independent entities will be those posited by physics. Perhaps we can invoke Locke's famous distinction between primary and secondary qualities and hold that only primary qualities of an object are mind-independent. There might be various ways that we try to distinguish between those things that exist mind-independently and those exist mind-dependently. This is something we will return to in Section 2.3. But, for now, to satisfy the independence commitment, it would be enough simply for some entity to be mind-independent, irrespective of whether we could come to *know* that entity is mind-independent.

Another way to make these somewhat vague comments more precise can be found in Page (2006). Page distinguishes between ontological, causal, structural, and individuative independence. Taking the first three together, an entity is ontologically independent if would continue to exist if there were no minds, causally independent if the entity were not brought into existence by the actions of a mind, and structurally independent if the entity has its structure independent of how we happen to talk or think about it. These three notions of independence might be endorsed by a realist, and some forms of anti-realism might deny one (or more) of these independence claims. Certain sorts of idealism, for example, might deny the ontological independence of entities; Goodman's worldmaking (under certain interpretations) would deny the structural independence of entities. However, as we will see in Section 3.3, there are anti-realists who accept ontological, causal, and structural independence.

It is individuative independence that is often taken to be most important for realism. The world is individuatively independent of us if 'it is divided up into individual things and kinds of things that are circumscribed by boundaries that are totally independent of where we draw the lines' (Page 2006: 327). This would mean that to be a realist is to believe that the world comes already divided up – that there are, to use another common metaphor, pre-existing, or objective 'joints' in nature that we, through our methods of investigation, hope or try to discover. Putnam echoes this idea when he states that one part of what it is to be a realist is to accept the view that 'the world divides itself up into objects and properties' (1992b: 123) and so does Sider (2011) who holds that an anti-realist is someone that holds that the world is not made of things, rather it is made of stuff, with the distinctions that we draw between entities being by fiat.

Of course, this relies on a certain conception of 'stuff' and one that not everyone accepts. Markosian (2015), for example, defends positing stuff in our ontology and holds that stuff makes up things. On Markosian's understanding of 'stuff', stuff can have properties that exist mind-independently. Others understand a stuff-ontology as a view that denies the existence of distinct individual objects. The world does not contain tables, chairs, and rocks under this view. Rather, the entities we typically think of as individual things are in fact patterns in the singular 'stuff' that really exists. What we think of as things might be mere patterns or modifications of this stuff, or bulges in space-time. Such views are straightforwardly realist, even if they are first-order realist views that posit fewer entities than other first-order realist views.

The sort of anti-realist stuff-ontology that Putnam and Sider have in mind, though, is different to this. The sort of view they have in mind does not posit stuff as composing things or posit stuff that might contain within it variations or patterns. They have in mind views that only posit undifferentiated stuff. Such views hold that there is a mind-independent world – it is not a form of idealism – but hold that the world is 'without kinds or order or motion or rest or pattern' (Goodman 1978: 20) or that the world is an amorphous lump (Dummett 1981; cf. Eklund 2008). Thus, a stuff-world is one that has no real or objective structure; there are no metaphysical joints or distinctions in reality itself. It is our language, thought, or concepts that carve up the otherwise undifferentiated world. Language, thought, or concepts are 'cookie cutters' that cut up and divide the amorphous lump reality. Properties, objects, things, and so on do not, therefore, exist mind-independently, not even as our way of talking about patterns or variations in the underlying 'stuff'. All distinctions that we make between entities (of any sort or kind) are solely based on our psychological, conceptual, or cultural biases, rather than being reflective of the world itself, and hence, no set of descriptions is *metaphysically* privileged in the sense of describing some mind-independent truth about the world.

Perhaps calling even this extreme form of a stuff-ontology anti-realist is too quick. It might be better to think of it as a very minimal form of realism. After all, it is realist in that it does posit the existence of a mind-independent world. However, it is only *minimally* realist as there is relatively little (if anything) that we can say about that mind-independent undifferentiated 'stuff'. And we might question whether positing a world of 'stuff' that contains no distinctions or variations – or at least none that is accessible to us – is sufficient for a view to be labelled realist. The answer to this, in my view, will depend on the third core commitment that we will turn to next: that of accessibility. If a stuff-ontology merely posits that there is some mind-independent stuff, but holds that reality is unknowable and undifferentiated, it has more in common with some views that are commonly classified as anti-realist.

Summarising, there were two key points to this discussion. First, the realist need not accept that *all* entities are mind-independent to be a realist. Nor that all aspects (or properties) of objects need be mind-independent – only that *some* are. Second, realists tend to be committed to the view that the world is pre-ordered or structured before we come to investigate it. There are mind-independent or objective 'joints in nature' that we (try to) discover. The entities that exist are thus individuatively independent.

Before moving on, there are three further important caveats. First, I have phrased my discussion as being about *mind*-independence for ease of exposition. But independence as a general criterion of realism is best understood as independence not just from minds but also from theories, thought, and/or language. The independence criterion is intended to capture the idea that the entities that the realist posits have their nature not due to any ways that we might represent them. Hence, from here on, I will talk simply about 'independence' as a shorthand for 'mind-, theory-, and language-independence'.

Second, it is important that any understanding of independence is not individualistic or human-specific. The intended independence is from *all* minds, both currently known and unknown. Realism would be shown to be false if it were discovered that all entities exist (or have their nature) in virtue of some advanced alien species with much greater but finite cognitive powers than us. Realism cannot be parochial – it is a claim about the independence of entities from our minds as they are, and also from minds with extended cognitive powers.

Third, understanding realism as being committed to independence says nothing about the existence (or non-existence) of mind-dependent (or human-dependent) entities, such as countries, borders, sports teams, and money. It is perfectly consistent with metaphysical realism to think that there are such entities and to think that any complete account of what exists includes those entities. Nothing in this outline of metaphysical realism commits the supporter of the view to the claim (or the denial of the claim) that *only* mind-independent entities exist.

Somewhat related to this, if we accept that at least some ways of dividing the world are socially constructed need not commit us to anti-realism either. A social constructivist might deny that there are 'natural kinds', but they do not (necessarily) deny that the world (and the objects in the world) have mind-independent properties. For example, although a border between two countries might be socially constructed, a realist (in our sense) may still maintain that there are genuine objects – for example, a river or mountain – that are independent in the requisite sense for realism. Nor would holding that the categorisation of an object can change lead us to anti-realism. How we categorise entities might change, while the mind-independent entities remain unchanged.

The way in which social entities' natures might depend on human beliefs, representations, or activities is a complex issue, and there is an ongoing debate about a more local form of realism concerned specifically with social entities. But this is not the focus here. For realism, in our sense, what is 'independent' can be more minimal. Merely the object existing and having *some* property would suffice (or even less is needed if we also believe that objects can exist without instantiating any property). There is no tension between being a social constructivist about some entity or entities and being a metaphysical realist, and nor must the metaphysical realist take a position on the existence of natural kinds or social entities to be classified as a realist.

This section has explored the ways in which people have argued that independence might be an important part of our characterisation of realism. Although providing a precise definition of independence has, as we have seen, proved to be difficult, we can reasonably take independence and existence to be necessary commitments of realism. As we have also noted, though, this is still quite a minimal form of realism, committing us not to the existence of any particular mind-independent entity or entities, only that there is *some* mind-independent entity (or that some aspect of an entity is mind-independent).

Furthermore, existence and independence do not (even taken together) commit the realist to any view about whether we can *say* or *know* about the mind-independent world. A view that accepts that there is a mind-independent world but holds that the world is in principle inaccessible to us would be a realist view if this combination were all there is to realism. As it happens, though, most realists think that we can know or talk meaningfully about the mind-independent world. This is not currently captured by our realist commitments, so something more is needed. The precise nature of this additional element varies, but all are some version of (what I will call) the *accessibility* commitment.

2.3 Accessing Reality

To understand the third potential commitment that is required to be a realist, it is useful to briefly comment on some history of philosophy. For a long time, realism was typically contrasted with views that denied one of the above-mentioned commitments. Opponents to realism either endorsed (external-world) scepticism (as the denial of the existence claim; see Section 3.1) or idealism (as a denial of the independence claim; see Section 3.2). This is why Davidson and Putnam write:

> [m]any philosophers believe antirealism to be a relatively recent metaphysical doctrine, certainly not endorsed by any thinker prior to Kant.
>
> (Davidson 1991: 147)

> [antirealism] is a late arrival in the history of philosophy, and even today it keeps being confused with other points of view of a quite different sort.
>
> (Putnam 1981: 49)

Kant is significant as he rejects metaphysical realism, but not through denying existence or independence. Kant's work shows that while existence and independence might be necessary for realism, they are not sufficient and, as the previous quotes suggest, result in Kant having a claim to be the first 'anti-realist'. So what part of realism does Kant reject if not existence or independence?

Kant (1997) writes:

> Long before Locke's time, but assuredly since him, it has generally been assumed that and granted without detriment to the actual existence of external things, that many of their predicates may be said to belong not to the things in themselves, but to their appearances, and to have no proper existence outside our representation. Heat, colour, and taste, for instance, are of this kind. Now, if I go further, and for weighty reasons rank as mere appearance the remaining qualities of bodies also, which are called primary, such as extension, place, and in general space, with all that which belongs to it (impenetrability or materiality, space, etc) – no one in the least can adduce the reason of its being inadmissible ... All the properties which constitute the intuition of a body belong merely to its appearance.
>
> (Prolegomena, section 13, remark II)

In Kantian terms, this is a rejection of the idea that we can have knowledge of the noumena – of things-in-themselves. The noumena is contrasted with the sensible world as the world of appearances (the phenomenal realm).

Unlike figures such as Locke, Kant places *all* properties that we can be aware of, including those that are the necessary conditions for thought (such as space and time), within the realm of 'appearances'. In so doing, Kant is rejecting the idea that we can, by any method, come to know about things-in-themselves – entities have 'no proper existence outside of our representation'.

Importantly, though, Kant is *not* denying that there is an external reality. He accepts that there is a mind-independent world. What he denies is that we could come to *know* about such a world. This is, ultimately, an epistemological claim in that our ability to know is limited to facts about phenomena, with the noumena (the mind-independent world) rendered inaccessible.

Kant scholarship is a difficult task, and this is not the place to engage in it. The above may not be the correct interpretation – for example, Langton (1998) argues that Kant held that it was (only) the intrinsic properties of objects that are unknowable and that the substances that possess those properties are able to affect us due to their causal powers. But it is an influential reading, and one that has had a major effect on how realism is characterised and the ways in which it might be rejected.

Davidson and Putnam both identify Kant as significant to the development of anti-realism. Prior to Kant, debates centred on questions about *how* we come to know about the world and what sorts of *things* the world contained. The major figures of early modern European philosophy disagreed not about whether they could come to know the nature of the world but about whether rational or empirical methods would provide such knowledge and whether material objects existed or not.

From Kant onwards, debates about realism take on an epistemological gloss. Rather than asking if there is an external world, post-Kant the question is: is there some way that we can reliably and informatively talk about reality? By answering this question negatively, the anti-realist does not doubt the existence of an external reality. Instead, significantly due to the influence of Kant, it is this question of *accessing* reality that dominates the realism debate in the twentieth century. Without pre-empting the discussion in Section 3.3 too much, in the post-Kant philosophical world, the arguments against metaphysical realism have focused on claims that the realist provides no satisfactory answer to the epistemic problems concerning how we might access reality, and, hence, realism fails. Thus, the third commitment required for realism, in addition to existence and independence, is what we can label the 'accessibility' commitment.

What, though, does this accessibility commitment consist of? So far, I have only told how Kant might have been influential for its introduction, but we have not outlined more precisely what it actually is. A first way of understanding accessibility, nicely summarised by Wright, is that realism requires some *fit* between the world and our language (or thoughts or concepts):

> A reasonable pre-theoretical characterization of realism about, say, the external world seems to me that it is a fusion of two kinds of thoughts, one kind expressing a certain modesty, the other more presumptuous. The modest kind of thought concerns the *independence* of the external world . . . that it is as it is independently of the conceptual vocabulary in terms of which we think about it, and that it is as it is independently of the beliefs about it which we do, will, or ever form . . ..
>
> The presumptuous thought, by contrast, is that while such fit as there may be between our thought and the world is determined independently of human cognitive activity, we are nevertheless, in favourable circumstances, capable of conceiving the world aright, and, often, of knowing the truth about it.
>
> (Wright 1992b: 1–2)

What Wright here describes as a 'fit' between the world and our thoughts is what I have been calling accessibility. It is the idea that in addition to there being a mind-independent world, we can know something about it or can state truths about it.

A realist might wonder why this additional commitment is needed at all. Could we not simply assert that realism is just a combination of existence and independence and hold that the ability for us to access mind-independent reality is some additional claim and is not part of the core commitments of realism? We certainly *could* do this. Devitt states something at least close to this when he says that there is 'epistemology lurking in the background' (1991: 4) of anti-realist arguments.

But, even if we are wary of this 'lurking' epistemology (a concern I am not entirely unsympathetic to this myself (see Miller 2014: chapter 1), I think there are good reasons to reject Devitt's concerns. This is because merely positing the existence of mind-independent entities feels insufficient for metaphysical realism and leads to the incorrect categorisation of certain views (Miller 2016). If realism consists in holding that there is a mind-independent world, but it turns out that we cannot know or say anything about that mind-independent world, it would make realism unimportant and uninteresting. Realism needs to be more than merely a promissory note, or a wave of the hand saying that there are mind-independent entities, but there is no way of knowing about them. More is needed for realism than positing that there is some inaccessible and unknowable world of entities 'out there'.

In addition to this, there are concerns that without something more, the claims of realism will end up being nonsensical. If realist claims are about the nature of mind-independent entities, but those entities are in principle inaccessible, then the claims of the realist will be 'devoid of cognitive content' (Carnap 1963: 868; see also Section 3.3.1). Realism without something to ensure that our language connects with the world feels empty. Or, as Button puts it: 'If the objects of the world are (largely) independent of our minds, languages, and theories, we need to know how we are able to think, speak, and theorize about them' (2013: 8).

What the realist therefore needs is some *access* to reality itself, or the ability to *know* about the nature of those mind-independent entities. This is what Thomasson calls 'epistemic realism': a commitment to the view 'that facts about the world are genuinely discoverable through substantive investigation subject to possibilities of confirmation and error, not just imposed by or to be read off of our concepts or beliefs' (2003: 582). Putting this another way, what the realist needs is some way for our language/concepts/thought to match or correspond to the mind-independent world. This does not mean that the realist is required to know *everything* about those entities or indeed that the realist at this moment in time knows anything certain about their nature. But the *possibility* of knowing – or put (yet) another way, that the nature of our language or thought does not *rule out* knowing – is taken to be important for realism.

Accessibility as stated so far is admittedly vague, and various means have been proposed to secure access. The rest of this section outlines some of the most prominent ideas. Though I have mentioned some reasons why the realist might feel the need to accept an accessibility claim, we should note that many of the specific views I will outline in the rest of this section have been introduced as purported commitments of realists by anti-realists, who subsequently argue that it is in virtue of these commitments that realism is flawed. Thus, while I do think that the realist needs something that ensures our claims that purport to be about the mind-independent world can (at least in principle) be true (or meaningful), it is notable that many of the most discussed ways to explicate accessibility in more detail are precisely those that anti-realists have problematised.

2.3.1 Truth

It is a common thread in the realism literature to hold that there is a connection between certain theories of truth and realism. Dummett writes that 'the dispute [between realists and anti-realists] thus concerns the notion of truth appropriate for statements of the disputed class' (1978: 146); Asay (2011: 189) argues that historically at least the theory of truth that was accepted often presupposed a position on the realist/anti-realist spectrum; and Putnam states that '[t]hat one could have a theory of truth which is neutral with respect to epistemological questions, and even with respect to the great metaphysical issue of realism versus idealism, would have seemed preposterous to a nineteenth-century philosopher' (1978: 9) and that 'Truth involves some sort of correspondence relation between words or thought-signs and external things and sets of things' (1981: 49). The debate about realism has thus often, implicitly or explicitly, been thought to be at the mercy of a proxy debate about what is the correct theory of truth. Realism, and by extension anti-realism were, in effect, defined through the adopted theory of truth. In slogan form: truth is non-neutral towards realism, and, more specifically, the claim is that a correspondence theory of truth presupposes and is a required part of realism and a rejection of correspondence leads to anti-realism.

There is a lot that could be said about what correspondence theory involves (for those interested, a good place to start is David 2018), but here we only need a simplified version. Under a correspondence theory of truth, truth consists in a relation between our representations and the world (or some portion of the world). A proposition (or sentence or some other truth bearer) is true if it 'matches' (or 'corresponds' or 'is isomorphic with', etc.) some fact (or state of affairs, or objects, or properties, etc.).

It is not hard to see why there is thought to be this connection between truth as correspondence to realism. A correspondence theory of truth posits a direct connection between our language (or concepts or representations) and the world. The correspondence theory of truth therefore seemingly provides the realist with exactly the 'access' that they might need. If assertions are true when they correspond to reality, then we have epistemic access to reality simply by working out what propositions are true. If the proposition 'the ball is red' is true, and truth involves correspondence with the world, then the proposition is true because there is some mind-independent entity that is a ball, which instantiates the property of redness. There remains the task to work out *which* propositions are true, but this would at least allow a method for realists to be able to hold that we can coherently talk/theorise about the nature of mind-independent entities.

If we accept that correspondence is required for realism, then it is common to also hold that non-correspondence theories, especially the coherence theory of truth, are a requirement for anti-realism. Under a coherence view, '"Truth" . . . is some sort of (idealized) rational acceptability – some sort of ideal coherence of our beliefs with each other and with our experiences as those experiences are themselves represented in our belief system' (Putnam 1981: 49–50; see also Walker 2018). Prima facie, this is inconsistent with the existence of an epistemically accessible mind-independent world that realism requires. Or at least knowing that something is true under this account would not give us any knowledge about the nature of mind-independent entities. The debate between the realist and the anti-realist thus might turn out to really be a debate about which theory of truth to accept.

Another influential possible connection between truth and realism is found in the work of Dummett (see his 1978, 1982, 1993). For Dummett, the realist is committed to the law of bivalence: the view that all meaningful statements are either true or false. This is contrasted with the idealist, who, Dummett argues, will reject bivalence. I will return to this connection later in Section 3.3.1, but it is worth noting that it is this that leads Dummett to argue that the realism–idealism debate can be reduced to a debate about what laws of logic are accepted and hence is not a deeper metaphysical dispute about whether there exist (or not) mind-independent entities.

Although a connection between realism and truth is intuitive, it is not accepted by all. For example, some have argued that the correspondence theory of truth is not sufficient for realism (see Devitt 1991; Horwich 1996). The argument holds that correspondence makes no claim on reality itself. That is, we might accept that truth is correspondence but subsequently hold that there exist no entities and hence no truths as there is nothing for truths to correspond to. This would mean that the correspondence theory of truth is 'still distant from Realism, because it is silent on the existence dimension' (Devitt 1991: 42).

Putting this another way, the thought is that we can only derive realism from correspondence if we assume a significant realist premise: that certain entities do in fact exist. This shows that the correspondence theory is in fact insufficient for realism as to derive realism, we must first assume that the sorts of entities that our true claims correspond to are those the sort of mind-independent entities that the realist will endorse. As Devitt puts it: '[we] have derived Realism from a Correspondence Truth by adding half of it [i.e., realism] to a Correspondence Truth' (Devitt 1991: 42).

Concerns about the inability of theories of truth to distinguish between realism and anti-realism have led some to point towards *truthmaking* as being able to provide a better distinction. The truthmaker principle, at its most basic, holds that for some truth bearer to be true, it must be true in virtue of some entity – there is something that makes the proposition true.

For many, a commitment to truthmaking implies a realist position. For example, Bigelow states: 'I have sometimes tried to stop believing in the Truthmaker axiom. Yet I have never really succeeded. Without some such axiom, I find I have no adequate anchor to hold me from drifting onto the shoals of some sort of pragmatism or idealism. And that is altogether uncongenial to me; I am a congenital realist about almost everything' (1988: 123).

Heil describes truthmaking as a 'central tenet of realism' (2003: 61). The connection here is again quite natural. Truthmaking focuses on the task of identifying the entities that make some truth true, and it is natural to then think of those truthmakers as being part of reality in line with metaphysical realism. Or, as Armstrong understands the view, 'a truthmaker for a particular truth, then, is just some existent, some portion of reality, in virtue of which that truth is true', and 'to demand truthmakers for particular truths is to accept a realist theory for these truths' (2004: 5).

There are, though, some problems with using truthmaking to characterise realism. First, some versions of truthmaking (e.g., Armstrong's) are sometimes taken to just be a version of correspondence theory (though see McGrath 2003). If this is the case, the same worries that were raised previously about using it to characterise realism are inherited. If to accept truthmaking we need to hold that there are 'portions of reality' that make propositions true, then truthmaking would also be insufficient for realism.

Separately, Daly (2005) and Pendlebury (2010) have argued that a commitment to truthmaking is also not sufficient for realism as the truthmaking principle is compatible with views that traditionally are taken to be in opposition to realism, such as idealism or pragmatism. If this is right, then a commitment to truthmaking would tell us nothing about whether someone is a realist or not and would be of no use when we are trying to define or characterise realism.

This is not to say that truthmaking might not still have a use in this debate though. Asay (2012) has suggested that truthmaking allows us to focus on the nature of the entities posited as truthmakers and not directly on whether there are true claims being asserted. Realism, under this conception, is not about what theory of truth you accept but about the nature of the entities that you posit as truthmakers for true claims. Thus, the difference between idealism and realism lies in that the former posits mental states as truthmakers for claims, while the latter posits mind-independent entities.

This proposal, though, does not so much *define* realism as much as encourage those engaging in this debate to focus on the metaphysical issues over the epistemological. This approach therefore might be better as a tool to categorise views as realist, idealist, or anti-realist and not a further commitment that unifies all realists (Miller 2014).

2.3.2 Semantics

Accessibility suggests that the realist needs to posit some connection between the world and our representations of the world. Though the most discussed is truth, there are other possible connections that have been proposed.

Putnam, for example, suggests that a realist is committed to a particular view on the nature of meaning (or 'content' or 'semantics'; see Putnam 1981: 49). This amounts to the view that the realist is committed to semantic externalism: the 'view that (some) semantic properties of a subject's words and/or thoughts depend for their individuation on features of the subject's "external" environment' (Goldberg n.d.; see also Kallestrup 2011). Putnam also sometimes phrased this in terms of reference, with realism requiring that there 'is a determinate reference relation which holds between expressions of our language and the parts of the world to which they refer' (Fletcher 2016: 41).

A commitment to semantic externalism or determinate reference relations is suggested as it would ensure that our expressions 'match up' with the mind-independent entities posited by the realist. Of course, merely appealing to a reference relation that holds between our words (or thoughts) and the world will not be enough. It will rightly be asked as to *how* our language comes to stand in this relation with parts of the world. Here, there are various options for the realist depending on various additional commitments on other questions. Button (2013: chapter 3) offers a good discussion of various ways that the reference relation might be cashed out in more detail, though he argues against them all.

Whether the realist posits a correspondence theory of truth, accepts truth-making, or adopts a particular semantic theory, in each case, what is being defended is a way that the realist can 'access' the mind-independent world. Each, if successful, provides the realist with a way to link our representations to the mind-independent world, thereby ensuring that those entities are not *merely* 'out there' and that something true or meaningful can be said *about* them. Some account of *how* we can talk or think sensibly about the mind-independent world is therefore a reasonable addition to our list of core commitments of realism.

Given this, just as we have noted that a route to reject realism would be to reject either (or both) existence or independence, a third way is to argue that the nature of our language will reveal that realism is ill-founded and rests on an implausible conception of truth or on a flawed semantic theory. Indeed, as will be discussed in Section 3.3, this is perhaps the most common way of rejecting realism in the contemporary literature.

2.4 Uniqueness and Pluralism

Though less talked about, there is one last commitment of realism that needs to be mentioned. It is captured by Putnam who writes that for the realist, 'there is exactly one true and complete description of "the way the world is"' (1981: 49). This amounts to a *uniqueness* claim. Realism requires that there is a *singular* or *privileged* correspondence between the terms of a theory and the objects and the properties to which they refer (see Putnam 1981: 49; see also Button 2013: 7–11). There are various other concepts that are used to express similar ideas in the literature: Dasgupta talks of the 'eliteness' of certain terms (2018), Sider of 'joint-carving notions' (2011), and Lewis of 'perfectly natural' properties (1983a; though see Lewis 2009 for a shift in his view).

Whatever the terminology used, the central idea is that not only is there a connection between our representations and the world but that some representations (or descriptions) are more accurate to, or better reflect, the objective sameness and difference found in nature. This needs to be sharply distinguished from how *useful* the descriptions might be. The anti-realist can accept that some terms or concepts are more or less useful. But, while the realist grounds their separation of the more or less natural (or more or less elite, etc.) in the world, the anti-realist will ground any such divisions in how we happen to choose to classify the world (see Taylor 1993). The realist and anti-realist begin to come apart therefore on whether they accept that there can be a way to classify the world that is uniquely 'best', where 'best' is understood not through some pragmatic criteria, but as being determined by the ability of that classification to capture objective sameness and difference in the world.

If we accept this uniqueness requirement, then the realist needs to have some way to be able to distinguish between those terms that are more and less accurate to reality, including potentially those that perfectly correspond. Uniqueness requires that the realist thinks that whatever the content of the description might be, there is some privileged or metaphysically 'best' or 'ideal' way to describe mind-independent reality.

This is not to deny the fallibility of the realist's theories. It might be that our current best theory is, in fact, false. This is a possibility that drives some forms of anti-realism as will be discussed in Section 3.3.2. But, for now, it is only to note that the realist can allow that our current theories are not *the* metaphysically privileged theory and only requires that there (at least in principle) could be such a privileged theory.

Note also that this is not the trivial point that some word or term might have meant something different or that for certain purposes on certain occasions, multiple explanations for some phenomena might be equally useful. The debate concerns the denial of any privileged set of descriptions amongst sets of ontological expressions, and whether any might be privileged in a metaphysical sense, rather than some pragmatic sense. This means that the realist is being taken to be committed to something more like the view that there is a hierarchy of expressive richness in relation to the world and that that hierarchy includes at least the potential for a language that only uses 'perfectly joint-carving' terms, or terms that refer to only 'perfectly natural' properties. Many anti-realists deny this, holding that there is no such hierarchy between competing metaphysical accounts of the nature of reality, or argue that there are many equally good descriptions, with only pragmatic reasons to choose between them.

Understanding this commitment helps illustrate the connection between uniqueness and accessibility. One way, as will be seen in Section 3.3, to deny accessibility will be to argue against there being any coherent sense of a 'uniquely privileged' description of reality. If there is no metaphysically 'best' way to describe the world, then, it will be argued, there is no good reason to suppose that we are 'accessing' or describing reality at all.

Uniqueness, though, should be distinguished from pluralism. Previously, I described uniqueness as being a debate between realists who think there is one privileged way to describe reality and anti-realists who hold that there are multiple equally good ways to describe reality. On first reading, this might appear to cast metaphysical (or ontological) pluralism as a form of anti-realism as the metaphysical pluralist argues that there are multiple ways of being and hence may accept that there are multiple equally good ways to describe reality (see McDaniel 2017; Turner 2010). But this form of pluralism is a form of realism. The difference is that the anti-realist position argues that there are at least two different languages, or different sets of ontological expressions, that are expressively equal or truth-conditionally equivalent, while the ontological pluralist, in contrast, can accept that there is a single uniquely privileged description of reality, but it just happens to be the case that description includes a pluralistic notion of 'being'.

2.5 Why Accept Realism?

We have covered what commitments metaphysical realism might involve, but why should we accept realism? Unlike other forms of realism, such as scientific realism, moral realism, aesthetic realism, and so on, there are surprisingly few explicit arguments *for* metaphysical realism. Rather, metaphysical realism is often defended as being the default view and a general sense that while the world might trick us (hence why there are sceptical scenarios to consider; see Section 3.1), it cannot be the case that the world tricks us *entirely*. Smart makes this point nicely (he is talking about scientific beliefs, but his point relates to realism as the acceptance that there is a mind-independent reality):

> Part of the point of my use of the example against Putnam is that all methodological constraints (especially Ockham's Razor) should lead us to deny that it was true. So if it were true the universe would trick us. I believe

that the universe probably does trick us in various ways. I say this because of my empirical beliefs about scientific methodology and about the human cognitive apparatus. However there would be a pragmatic paradox in my believing that it is physically possible that the main core of my scientific beliefs might be wrong. This is because it is this core of scientific beliefs that gives me my notion of what is physically possible. (1986: 311)

Similarly, Devitt calls realism the 'common-sense' view and says that it is 'almost universally accepted outside of intellectual circles' (2008: 226). Sider describes his commitment to realism as being 'knee-jerk', where:

Knee-jerk realism is a vague picture rather than a precise thesis. According to the picture, the point of human inquiry – or a very large chunk of it anyway, a chunk that includes physics – is to conform itself to the world, rather than to make the world. The world is 'out there', and our job is to wrap our minds around it. This picture is perhaps my deepest philosophical conviction. I've never questioned it; giving it up would require a reboot too extreme to contemplate; and I have no idea how I'd try to convince someone who didn't share it. (2011: 18)

(Note that Sider ties his 'knee-jerk' realism to a *physicalist* thesis (2011: 19–20), but these aspects can come apart; see Irmak 2013 and Miller 2021 for discussion.)

The realist therefore takes their position to be the starting point or to be the intuitively correct view. Such an approach puts the ball in the anti-realist court. It is not for the realist to defend realism, initially at least. It is for the anti-realist to propose reasons why something so ordinary or mundane as the existence and accessibility of a mind-independent world should be rejected. Of course, for anybody not already committed to realism, accepting a view simply because it fits with our intuitive view of the world may not be something that many are willing to do. Philosophers often revel in rejecting 'common-sense' views, or at least problematising them, so even if realism is the intuitive position, this may not persuade many to accept realism.

2.6 Taking Stock

Let us take stock. Various concepts have been introduced in this section in an attempt to specify the core commitments of realism. The most minimal commitments are existence and independence, but these are normally added to, with the realist also taken to hold that we can meaningfully or truthfully say something about (the nature of) the mind-independent world. We have also seen that realism is sometimes associated with a uniqueness claim – that some description of reality is uniquely privileged or accurate when compared to competing descriptions.

As noted previously, we have not in this Element covered the debates about what sort of entity the realist thinks exists. Under the offered characterisation, a realist is committed to the mind-independent existence of some *entity*, and some further accessibility requirement to allow us to come to know something about the properties or nature of that *thing*. The more specific details – whether that *entity* is a property, event, process, object, cause, law of nature, particular, universal, and so on – is a further matter and one that realists will disagree over. This (hopefully) provides a broad characterisation of realism that will allow us, in the next section, to consider the arguments against realism via the denial of one (or more) of these commitments.

I want to finish this section with one last consideration that will become important as this Element progresses. How we define realism, and whether we accept or reject it, will have consequences on how we view metaphysical debates more widely. What will emerge in the next section is that the range of views that reject realism vary widely, with a particularly important difference between views that combine their rejection of realism with a rejection of *metaontological realism* and those that do not.

Put briefly, metaontological realists hold that (at least some) metaphysical (and ontological) disputes are substantive. That is, that when we do metaphysics, we are engaging in a practice that at least *could* arrive at claims about the nature of fundamental reality or help us understand the essence of the entities under discussion. In contrast, *metaontological* anti-realism is the view that all (or most) metaphysical (and ontological) disputes are non-substantive. Metaphysical disputes are shallow, pointless, or merely verbal (see Jenkins 2010).

Depending on what commitments we take to be required for realism, being a realist can be combined with either metaontological realism or anti-realism. For example, if we take realism to be minimal – that is, just a combination of existence and independence – we can accept idealism while being a metaontological realist (see Section 3.2). On the other hand, if we take realism to require some accessibility commitment and we reject realism, this is typically also combined with metaontological anti-realism (as is the case in much of the contemporary arguments against realism; see Section 3.3).

This is at least one place where views on what the commitments of realism are have further consequences. Different metaontological positions can be combined with realism (or the rejection of realism) depending on whether we take realism to be 'merely' the commitment to their being mind-independent entities or if we take realism to also require that we can access those mind-independent entities. And the influence could also be in the opposite direction: if we have strong views about metaontological realism/anti-realism and the substantivity of metaphysical disputes, this could influence which forms of metaphysical realism (or anti-realism) are plausible.

3 Rejecting Realism

If realism is some combination of the commitments discussed in Section 2, it is natural that opponents of realism generally deny one (or more) of these. This section will discuss some families of arguments against realism while noting some prominent lines of response.

A note of terminology: in the previous section, I largely used the term anti-realism for any view that is opposed to realism. In this section, I follow others (e.g., Davidson 1991: 147; Putnam 1981: 49) in labelling only some of these views as 'anti-realism'. More precisely, I will take realism to stand in opposition to three distinct families of views: scepticism, idealism, and anti-realism, with each of these characterised as involving the denial of a different realist commitment. This is naturally something of a simplification, and some views deny multiple realist commitments. However, I hope that this structure best allows the reader new to this topic to see the differences between some of the most common arguments against realism.

3.1 Denying 'Existence': (Radical) Scepticism

Holding that nothing exists is certainly counter-intuitive, and for many throughout history, the need to explicitly commit to the existence of reality was not apparent. Indeed, one anonymous reviewer for this Element suggested that denying the existence of the world as a way of responding to realism was like using a sledgehammer to crack a nut. This is true in many ways, and certainly denying the existence commitment is the least common route to rejecting realism.

However, there are those that would reject the existence commitment and two ways of doing so that have been particularly influential. The first route is directly metaphysical (or ontological), while the second is epistemic (or sceptical). In both cases, it is important to stress that the intended denial of the existence of reality is global in scope. This means that the sort of view of interest here is not merely the view that there are a lot fewer objects than we typically think (e.g. eliminativism or reductionism about tables, chairs, and the like), nor the view that the world contains only 'stuff' (cf. Section 2.2.2), and nor is it the view that the best language to describe reality does not use 'feature-placing terms' (see O'Leary-Hawthorne and Cortens 1995; Turner 2011). Rather, the views of interest here deny the existence of everything. To deny the existence commitment of realism is to hold 'that there are no objects, no properties, no events, no space–time, no structures, no facts or states of affairs, no appearances, no anything' (Westerhoff 2021: 2).

We will begin with the metaphysical variant: 'ontological nihilism'. The ontological nihilist argues that there are good metaphysical arguments to the conclusion that nothing exists. This is not, like the sceptic below, an epistemic claim about our ability to *know* something about reality. Nihilism instead directly argues against all existence claims asserted by the realist. That is, the nihilist will argue that for any entity, x, for which we might ask 'Does x exist?' we should simply answer 'no'. Ontological nihilism denies existence, but in so doing, it also leads to a denial of other commitments of realism: if nothing exists, then it follows that there cannot be anything that exists mind-independently, thereby denying independence, and nor is there any thing to access, denying accessibility.

Why might we accept ontological nihilism? The view has not attracted much support in the Western philosophical tradition, nor do major historical figures in the Western tradition spend much time considering and rejecting the view. But ontological nihilism is more prominent in certain parts of Buddhist philosophy, in particular in Madhyamaka philosophy and the work of Nāgārjuna. Though this interpretation is a matter of debate (see Spackman 2014; Westerhoff 2016), here is a very quick sketch of a version of ontological nihilism (possibly) found in Nāgārjuna.

In Buddhist philosophy, there is a distinction between primary existents – irreducible, objective elements of the world – and secondary existents – those entities that depend on our representative practices (Westerhoff 2018). Primary existents, under non-nihilist views, provide a foundation for secondary existents. However, Nāgārjuna denies that there is any ontological foundation to the world. This is because he denies the primary existents lack any 'svabhāva' – roughly any intrinsic nature or substance. If primary existents lack svabhāva, it is possible to read Nāgārjuna as denying their existence, and it follows from this that we must also deny the existence of secondary existents. Hence, we arrive at ontological nihilism. For those interested in a more detailed discussion of Nāgārjuna's views, including those that would deny this reading, Garfield (2005), Westerhoff (2018), and Siderits and Katsura (2013) are good places to start.

Another argument for ontological nihilism can be found in Westerhoff (2021). Westerhoff argues that nihilism follows from a combination of two independently supportable claims: eliminativism and non-foundationalism. The idea, roughly, is that there are good independent arguments in favour of only fundamental entities existing (i.e., in support of eliminativism) *and* that there is no fundamental level of reality (i.e., in support of non-foundationalism). But, if these claims are accepted together, this provides a metaphysical argument for the conclusion that nothing exists as we have grounds to deny the existence of all fundamental and non-fundamental entities. We therefore again arrive at ontological nihilism, though we might alternatively view this as a reason to reject one of eliminativism and non-foundationalism.

Ontological nihilism faces a well-known inconsistency objection. If nihilism is true, then the thought 'nothing exists' must be true. But this implies that there exists a thought, and hence, nihilism is self-defeating. Or we can run the same line of argument about the *fact* that nothing exists. If nihilism is true, then this fact must obtain, and again nihilism seems to be shown to be false. See Westerhoff (2021: 3–4) for a possible line of response to these inconsistency arguments.

For most, though, it is the deeply counter-intuitiveness of ontological nihilism, and the extreme nature of the view, which means it is not generally considered plausible. Yes, if ontological nihilism is true, all forms of realism would be shown to be false. But at what cost? Idealism, and most other anti-realist views, would also need to be rejected. Denying the existence criterion is simply too high a price to pay just to reject realism and one that is not needed given the possibility of denying one (or both) of the other criteria outlined previously.

Let us move on to the epistemic route to deny existence, and a view that is likely more familiar to many readers: external-world or radical scepticism. Scepticism and realism have an uneasy relationship. On the one hand, realism has often been taken to require the possibility of scepticism or at least the coherency of sceptical concerns. The thought is that if sceptical concerns were not possible, then we would not be able to maintain or posit the appearance–reality distinction that the realist needs for the world to be truly mind-independent. On the other hand, though, a realist will want to resist global or radical scepticism. The radical sceptic argues that we can have no knowledge of any aspect of reality and hence that we have no good reason to posit that such a reality exists, something that the realist is clearly not going to agree with.

This means that the realist both wants to be able to allow the possibility of scepticism, at least on the local scale – for example, that the table in front of me may *really* just be particles-arranged-tablewise or even may not *really* exist – but rule out radical scepticism wherein *all* seemingly external entities do not exist. Sceptical arguments against realism often play on this tension and try to argue that there is no way for the realist to avoid the slippery slope between allowing a local scepticism about particular entities or in particular scenarios and a global scepticism that maintains that there is no such thing as an external world at all.

Versions of radical scepticism have a long history, and some forms of scepticism can be found in ancient Greek thought, the most famous being Sextus Empiricus, a Pyrrhonian sceptic who lived (probably) in the second or third century CE. However, there is a debate about the scope of ancient scepticism. For example, Burnyeat suggests that 'the Greeks never posed the problem of the existence of an external world in the general form we have known it since Descartes' (1982: 23; see also Adamson 2015: chapter 15). According to Burnyeat, Sextus' scepticism is limited to what Fine has labelled 'property scepticism', the view that there is an external world that contains familiar objects and that what should be doubted is that such objects have the properties that they appear to have (Fine 2003: 342).

Whether radical scepticism can be found in the ancient world or not, the most well-known discussion of radical scepticism in the Western philosophical world is undoubtedly found in the work of Descartes. Descartes is concerned with knowledge and our ability to know what is true. The world appears to us in a certain way, but we could be wrong about how it *really* is. We can recognise that our senses are commonly deceived in ordinary circumstances – a stick in a glass of water appears to be bent when we know it to be straight. But, if our senses are not reliable in those cases, why should we think them reliable in other cases? The world might be radically different from the way that it appears to us, and we cannot rule out that we might be dreaming or that an evil demon might be tricking us.

Different versions of radical scepticism can be found in many philosophical works and have made their way into our wider culture. How can we rule out that we are not dreaming (as is suggested in *Inception*) or that we are not all living in a computer simulation (as is suggested in *The Matrix*)? All of these amount to the same concern: how can we be sure about the accuracy of any of the ways in which we perceive the world? How, if at all, can we rule out that the world we perceive is nothing but appearances, with no reality beyond those appearances?

A multitude of responses to radical or global scepticism have been put forward. Descartes himself tries to solve his concerns via the notion of 'clear and distinct' ideas, and the certain, undoubtable knowledge of the cogito (though this solution faces the problem of the Cartesian Circle; see Hatfield 2006). Moore (1925, 1939) rejects scepticism in favour of a 'common sense' realist position and argues that radical sceptical positions are self-undermining. Moore argues that there are some things that cannot be intelligibly doubted, and hence, external-world scepticism must be false. Later, Moore (1959) argues that even if we cannot disprove scepticism, we are at least not rationally compelled to accept the sceptic's arguments as both the sceptical and non-sceptical arguments are valid. Neither side's arguments can be disproved because they rely on premises that the other side would view as question-begging, leaving the realist and the sceptic at an impasse. But such an impasse, for Moore, is still an achievement, for it means that we can accept the validity of the sceptic's arguments, without being forced to accept them. Still other responses draw on views and theories within epistemology to further clarify our understanding of justification, aiming to secure through that a way in which ordinary empirical claims about the external world can be justified (see Greco 2007). Even if these solutions work, however, there might be a deeper problem facing realism due to radical scepticism found in the work of Hilary Putnam.

Putnam first extends sceptical arguments against realism through his 'brain-in-a-vat' thought experiment. The most developed version of this thought experiment asks us to consider whether, for all we know, all sentient creatures might just be brains-in-a-vat, overseen and manipulated by some powerful machine. This certainly seems conceptually possible: due to the same appearance–reality distinction and sceptical worries that Descartes drew on, we cannot rule out the possibility straight away. Hence, Putnam's brains-in-a-vat first produce yet another sceptical scenario for the realist to contend with.

However, Putnam argues that this leads to a more serious problem for realism. This problem comes from the combination of the realist allowing that the 'brains-in-vats' scenario is a genuine possibility and the realist's independent commitment to semantic externalism: the view that the meaning of words is (at least) partially determined by the connection between the speaker and the world itself (see Section 2.3.2). For example, if semantic externalism is true, there is some connection between the word 'tree' and real trees (Putnam 1981: 12–13; see also Putnam 1975). For the realist, the meaning of words like 'tree' must be determined, at least in part, by the fact that the word refers to (or picks out) actual trees. This reference relation explains why the word 'table' means something different to the word 'tree'. 'Table' has a different meaning as the objects in the world that it refers to differ from those that the word 'tree' refers to.

Semantic externalism has consequences for the meaning of words for brains-in-a-vat. Brains-in-vats may have qualitatively identical thoughts and experiences to us, but those experiences are not connected to the external world. When a brain-in-a-vat says 'tree', there cannot be a reference relation between the word and actual trees as the brain-in-a-vat never experiences an actual tree. The brain-in-a-vat's experience is of a computer-generated simulation of a tree, and it is some aspect of that simulation that their word 'tree' will refer to. The word 'tree' when uttered (or thought) by a brain-in-a-vat cannot refer to a real tree. If semantic externalism is correct, then the word 'tree' when uttered by a brain-in-a-vat will have a different meaning than when uttered by those of us who are unvatted.

Now Putnam asks us to consider the question 'am I a brain-in-a-vat?' It appears that I can think this question because there exists the required connection between my words 'brain' and 'vat' to allow them to refer to real brains and real vats. But the same cannot be true of a brain-in-a-vat. For them, 'brain' and 'vat' *cannot* refer to a real brain or a real vat but only to some computer-generated simulation of brains and vats. Unlike us who are our unvatted brains, the brain-in-a-vat cannot even ask (or think) the question 'am I a brain-in-a-vat?' Our very ability to ask whether we are brains-in-vats shows that we cannot possibly be brains-in-a-vat. The conclusion is that the realist cannot maintain both that such sceptical scenarios are genuinely possible and accept semantic externalism. As Putnam argues in favour of semantic externalism (see Putnam 1975), it is realism that must be rejected. And, furthermore, as, at least according to Putnam, semantic externalism is a necessary part of realism, realism should not just be rejected; it is self-refuting.

The discussion of Putnam's brain-in-a-vat thought experiment has been extensive, and there is more than can be covered here. For more discussion, both in favour and against this argument, see (amongst many others) Goldberg (2015), Wright (1992a), and Brueckner (2010) . I will, though, briefly highlight two main lines of response that realists have tended to take.

First, the realist could deny semantic externalism in favour of another semantic theory (e.g., Horwich 1990; Lewis 1984; Resnick 1990). If there were some other robust reference relation holding between our words and the world, then the brain-in-a-vat argument would not endanger realism. However, note that a further major argument against realism proposed by Putnam, the model-theoretic argument, which will be discussed in Section 3.3.2, does not rely on semantic externalism and might block this route of response.

Second, the brain-in-vat argument concludes that realism (and semantic externalism) cannot be maintained alongside a commitment to the possibility of radical sceptical scenarios. It is therefore potentially open to the realist to simply deny the possibility of radical scepticism and the possibility of the brain-in-a-vat sceptical scenario also.

3.2 Denying 'Independence': Idealism

As with existence, an explicit commitment to independence by the realist is, in part, motivated by the development of views that deny this commitment, most centrally, idealism. Idealism as a term comes from the work of Wolff (1751) and idealism comes in many different forms, across many philosophical traditions.

Certainly missing many other examples, forms of idealism can be found in the Vedānta school of Hindu philosophy (see Hamilton 2001; King 1995), and the Lu-Wang School of Neo-Confucianism (see Ivanhoe 2009). Agada (2019, 2021) has recently argued for the importance of consolationism within the African philosophical tradition and has called this a form of 'African idealism'. In the Western philosophical tradition, often following and building on the work of Kant, there is the German idealism of Fichte, Schelling, and Hegel and the British–American idealism most associated with people such as Bradley, McTaggart, and Royce. Given all of these distinct forms of idealism, each stemming from their own complex philosophical traditions, to try to cover idealism as a whole would be well beyond the limits and scope of this Element.

Therefore, I will limit the discussion here to one form of idealism that has been particularly influential in debates about metaphysical realism. Guyer and Horstmann (2021) call this version 'metaphysical' or 'ontological idealism', as opposed to 'epistemological idealism' (which is closer in spirit to some of the views that will be discussed in Section 3.3). Ontological idealism is the view that everything that exists is (in some way) mental. There are no 'physical' entities existing outside of our experience of them, or as deVries puts it: 'Roughly, [idealism] comprises theories that attribute ontological priority to the mental, especially the conceptual or ideational, over the non-mental' (2009: 211). The idealist therefore accepts the existence requirement but rejects the independence criterion.

Ontological idealism finds its most famous supporter in the Western tradition in George Berkeley (though he labels his position 'immaterialism'). Berkeley holds that all that exists are minds and ideas, rejecting the existence of material objects entirely. Berkeley puts forward various arguments for idealism, both from an epistemic and metaphysical perspective, and argues against 'material-ism' as the view that material entities exist or, equivalently, that there are mind-independent entities. 'Materialism' is therefore the view that we have been calling 'realism'. (The range and complexity of Berkeley's arguments cannot be done justice here. For more detail see Berkeley 1948–1957; for good introduc-tions to Berkeley's idealism, see Rickless 2013; Winkler 1989.)

Berkeley (in part) argues against realism on the basis that only idealism can resolve the threat of scepticism. Berkeley argues that the materialist has no reliable way to distinguish between those 'true' properties of an object and those properties that we are misperceiving, thereby undermining the distinction present in Locke between primary and secondary qualities. The realist cannot explain why we should think that some properties, like colour or taste, are merely properties of perception, while other properties, such as weight and shape, are properties of mind-independent objects. In contrast, an idealist, says

Berkeley, can simply hold that *both* sorts of properties are mind-dependent. This provides a way to refute scepticism. As all properties, and indeed all entities, are mind-dependent, we can resist scepticism: our senses do not mislead us about the nature of material entities because there are no material entities.

Even this overly simplified description suffices for us to be able to easily see why Berkeleyan idealism is a common first view that people think of as an alternative to realism. Berkeley clearly cannot hold that there exists a *mind-independent* reality in that he holds that all that exists is mind-dependent. However, Berkeleyan idealism, nor idealism more generally, is not the normal territory for contemporary anti-realists. This is, I think, for two main reasons.

The first is the unpopularity of idealism in the contemporary (analytic) philosophical world. Indeed, refuting idealism (and scepticism) was one of the major aims of many important figures in the early parts of the twentieth century and at the emergence of the analytic tradition. For example, founding figures of analytic philosophy such as Moore (1899, 1903, 1925), Stebbing (1929, 1932–1933, 1942; see also Janssen-Lauret Forthcoming), and Russell (1912) all devote significant time to discussing the 'threat' of idealism, and their work has shaped the literature significantly even to this day (though we should note that Russell did also, at one time, defend idealism; see Griffin 1991; Hylton 1990). Even Carnap, one of the most significant anti-realists in the twentieth century, held that his work was 'neutral with respect to the traditional controversies, e.g., realism vs. idealism' in the sense that he saw his work as rejecting both (1963: 17–18).

This is not to deny that there are historical exceptions to this trend, such as Bradley (1897), McTaggart (1921–1927), and Royce (1919) and that some more recent defences can be found such as in Goldschmidt and Pearce (2017). But, while it would be false to say that idealism is 'dead', it is fair to say that it is not widely defended and not a major view within the realism/anti-realism literature today.

The second reason is related to the metametaphysical commitments of many contemporary anti-realists. The literature on realism has, for better or worse, largely shifted away from discussions of idealism and towards versions of anti-realism that also incorporate some form of metaontological anti-realism (see Section 2.6). Contemporary anti-realists tend to focus on concerns about the intelligibility of realism (and metaphysics more widely) that arise from the sorts of epistemological and semantic concerns that I grouped together under the accessibility commitment of realism.

Such concerns are not normally found in idealism, at least with respect to realism that is global in scope. Idealists may raise particular semantic or epistemic arguments against realism. Berkeley famously argues against the existence of material objects due to significant epistemological concerns combined with his commitment to empiricism. But Berkeley, taking him again as a classic example of an ontological idealist, does *not* deny that we can speak intelligibly about the nature of reality. Berkeley and a realist do not disagree about the existence of reality or our ability to know what it is like. Rather, the debate between the realist and the idealist is about what (kinds of) entities exist and whether reality contains material (or physical) objects or not.

What this shows is that the realist and (at least Berkeleyan) idealist share some significant metaontological common ground. Both argue that it is possible to discuss and describe the nature of reality. This, in my view, at least partly explains the unpopularity of idealism today as an alternative to realism. In so far as the realist disagrees with an idealist, this is not a disagreement about a global form of realism. It is a local first-order ontological disagreement about what exists. It is a disagreement about a *local* form of realism: about the existence (or not) of one particular kind of entity – material (or mind-independent) objects.

This leads to an interesting categorisation question: can we, in some sense, think of Berkeley as a realist? The sensible answer, I think, is still no. But recognising the fact that Berkeleyan idealism does not deny access to reality reiterates the connection between realism and debates in metametaphysics noted in Section 2.6. Unlike most forms of anti-realism that will be discussed in the next section, Berkeley's idealism is a *metaontological* realist position. This means that the Berkeleyan idealist does not doubt the coherency of metaphysics, nor our ability to know what fundamental reality is like. For the Berkeleyan idealist, mental entities are all that exist. This is compatible with the view that a description of such entities is a description of the fundamental structure of reality. This is still not a form of metaphysical realism as I have been characterising the view here – it still denies that there exist some entities that are *mind-independent*. But it is a metaontological realist position. In answering metaphysical questions, we are not merely revealing facts about how we happen to speak, think, or conceive of the world. We are making true claims about the nature of reality, and it just so happens that reality is populated solely by mind-dependent entities. This is in contrast to most contemporary forms of anti-realism which often combine a rejection of metaphysical realism with metaontological anti-realism, at least partly explaining why idealism is not seen as an attractive alternative to realism.

3.2.1 Irrealism

As noted previously, idealism is a less popular view than it once was, but one notable related view from the twentieth century deserves a specific mention and can serve as a useful bridging view between ontological idealism and contemporary anti-realism. In the foreword to his *Ways of Worldmaking*, Nelson Goodman writes:

> I think of this book as belonging in that mainstream of modern philosophy that began when Kant exchanged the structure of the world for the structure of the mind, continued when C. I. Lewis exchanged the structure of the mind for the structure of concepts, and that now proceeds to exchange the structure of concepts for the structure of the several symbol systems of the sciences, philosophy, the arts, perception, and everyday discourse. The movement is from unique truth and a world fixed and found to a diversity of right and even conflicting versions or worlds in the making. (1978: x)

When Goodman talks here, and elsewhere, of 'making' worlds, he means it literally: through our actions (most centrally thought and language), we *literally* create the world around us.

What, though, does it mean to literally create the world? To better understand Goodman, we should start with his rejection of there being some unifying neutral reality that makes true seemingly contradictory claims. Goodman rejects what he calls monism – the view that there is a single world – in part due to the truth of contradictory propositions such as 'The Sun never moves' and 'The Sun always moves'. For Goodman, both claims are true, but their truth leads to a puzzle about *how* they can both be true. He considers the idea that the world allows for multiple contrasting 'aspects'. Such aspects would make both claims true by relativising them to particular frames of reference. This would thereby allow both to be true of a single world.

But Goodman argues that the sheer variety of differing aspects make this move to explain contradictory truths implausible: 'we have no neat set of frames of reference, no ready rules for transforming physics, biology, and psychology into one another, and no way at all of transforming any of these into Van Gogh's vision, or Van Gogh's into Canaletto's' (1978: 3).

Putting this another way, the problem with an underlying neutral reality for Goodman is that such a view requires ultimately that truths in one domain be reduced or captured within another. But 'the evidence for such reducibility is negligible, and even the claim is nebulous since physics itself is fragmentary and unstable and the kind and consequences of reduction envisaged are vague. (How do you go about reducing Constable's or James Joyce's world-view to physics?)' (1978: 5).

Goodman therefore is rejecting the idea that differing descriptions are descriptions of the *same* world. There is no external mind-independent reality, and nor is there some unique set of truths made true by some pre-structured world. It is not, though, a view under which nothing exists. Things exist but they have their nature and structure due to us. For Goodman, we *make* the world.

Goodman's view therefore bears some similarities to idealism. However, it is unlike other forms of idealism: it denies that there is a single correct account of the world – something that Berkeley would have accepted due to the role of God in maintaining the world For Goodman, we actively make the world through our conceptualisations. With respect to our working conception of realism in this Element, Goodman accepts both existence and access but denies impendence – after all, how could those entities be mind-independent when we (creatures with minds) have literally made them.

Goodman's views are certainly unique, and though there has been lots of discussion (see Cohnitz and Rossberg 2006; Dudau 2002; Putnam 1992a), there has not been significant ongoing support for Goodman's irrealism, and Goodman's most major influence on the philosophical literature has been his work on induction (see Goodman 1955) and nominalism (see Goodman and Quine 1947). It is also worth noting that although I have included his world-making under the 'idealism' section, there are strong similarities to the sorts of views that will be discussed in the next section. Like Carnap and Putnam, for example, Goodman defends the anti-realist idea that there is no single object-ively best description of reality. The difference is that while Carnap and Putnam hold that those multiple descriptions are equally good descriptions of the *same* world, Goodman takes them to be descriptions of different worlds.

3.3 Denying 'Accessibility': Anti-realism

Thus far, we have considered views that deny existence and independence. However, many (even most) contemporary opponents to realism – arbitrarily taken to be those from roughly the second half of the twentieth century onwards – do not typically reject either of these commitments. This is not to say that there are no modern-day defences of ontological nihilism or idealism. It is only to say that the existence and independence commitments have not been the focus of those seeking to reject realism.

Instead, what is rejected by most contemporary responses to realism is the accessibility and/or the uniqueness commitments. This has been argued for in many ways, in part because (as we saw previously) these commitments were themselves less precise and more varied in how realism was taken to satisfy them. However, as will become clear, there will often be a common idea: that realism should be rejected because there can be no uniquely privileged description of reality (or no 'best' or 'ideal' description) or that multiple different competing accounts are 'equally good'.

3.3.1 Language, Semantics, and Anti-realism: Wittgenstein, Carnap, and Dummett

In the twentieth century, new arguments against realism began to develop. Many of these arguments rested on claims about the nature of language, holding that language is no 'mirror' on the world. Instead, language obscures, distorts, or even entirely restricts our attempts to describe (or describe objectively) the nature of reality. These arguments therefore reject the relationship between language and the world that is posited by the realist, thereby rejecting the accessibility commitment.

Famously, this interest in language was not isolated to debates about realism and was part of the wider 'linguistic turn' in philosophy. (Over)simplifying many aspects, the linguistic turn refers to a change in the subject matter of philosophical analysis. Prior to the linguistic turn, it was generally assumed that philosophical problems were about the *world* itself. After the turn, 'philosophical problems are problems which may be solved (or dissolved) either by reforming language, or by understanding more about the language we presently use' (Rorty 1992: 3). Or as Edmunds summarises:

> Language, of course, had always been the necessary apparatus with which to examine philosophical problems. But now language itself became the object of analysis. And whereas language had once been seen as a window between us and the world – clean, flat, and transparent – now it was treated with suspicion as grimy, warped, and opaque, requiring attention precisely because of the way it was capable of distorting or masking reality.
>
> (2020: chapter 4)

Language-focused anti-realist arguments draw on different elements of language, but most conclude that the realist 'produces sentences which fail to conform to conditions under which alone a sentence can be literally significant' (Ayer 1952: 35). Or, put another way, that statements purporting to be about the world that realists make (and argue about) are, due to the nature of language itself, ill-formed, empty of content, or meaningless.

Very often, these claims will not name their target as the 'realist' but as the 'metaphysician' or 'metaphysics' in general. For our discussion, though, we can take these terms to be synonymous in this context. For the conclusion of these arguments is both that realism is wrong and that metaphysical disputes, which are premised on accepting realism – for how can we sensibly debate the nature of certain entities if we do not presume some ability to talk about the mind-independent nature of those entities – are pointless or non-substantive.

We need to differentiate between weaker and stronger readings of these claims about language. The weaker reading holds that language might sometimes trick us or fail to be that clear window upon the world that we are seeking. Many (if not most) realists would accept this weaker claim, arguing that the 'ordinary' uses of terms are (often) insufficient for our aims and need to be replaced with more philosophically sophisticated alternatives. The realist may even characterise their role as being one of 'uncovering' or 'discovering' the metaphysically 'ideal' language – the language that 'carves nature at its joints' or 'ontologese'. Thus, whilst it is true that we cannot but use language as part of our investigation into the world, on the weaker reading, language is *not* the subject matter of our investigation. It is only the sometimes-flawed means through which we might communicate and theorise about reality itself. This weaker reading is entirely compatible with realism.

More interesting for this Element is the stronger reading that holds, for differing reasons, that language is in principle inadequate for the task of representing reality. Mind-independent entities may exist, but we cannot meaningfully talk about those entities because of the nature of language. The realist has been 'bewitched by language' and the problems the realist is concerned with only arise when 'language goes on holiday' (to borrow some Wittgensteinian phrases).

We should also make clear at this point that the term 'language' should not be read as referring to *specific* languages, either natural or formal. What follows are not claims about any particular language but about language as the set of all natural and formal languages that exist and are used and might come into existence at later times.

So why might we think that an investigation into the nature of language rules out realism? This could easily be the topic of its own book. Here, I will limit the discussion to arguments found in the work of three major figures – Wittgenstein, Carnap, and Dummett – who each put forward language (and/or logic) based arguments against realism.

Wittgenstein: Meaning as Use, and Language-Games

Wittgenstein scholarship is notoriously complex and intricate, especially when it concerns his 'early work'. Some argue that in the *Tractatus Logico-Philosophicus* (*TLP*), we find the same core anti-metaphysical themes that come to the fore in Wittgenstein's later work. Others argue the opposite: that in the early work, there is some acceptance of at least the coherence of metaphysical realism, even if a more sceptical attitude towards our ability to answer metaphysical questions than is found in the work of those that the *TLP* is significantly responding to (such as Russell and Frege). However the *TLP* is read, it is undeniable that there is a highly influential critique of metaphysics (and realism) in the 'later Wittgenstein' and in particular in the *Philosophical Investigations* (*PI*). I will therefore mainly focus on the *PI*. Those after a more in-depth and systematic discussion of Wittgenstein's evolving views on language, metaphysics, and realism, see, inter alia, Kuusela and McGinn (2011); McGinn (1997); McNally (2017); and Stern (2004).

Between the *TLP* and the *PI*, Wittgenstein's conception of language changes significantly and in ways that shift him away from realism and towards antirealism. In the *TLP*, Wittgenstein (appears to) posit mind-independent entities, such as states of affairs, objects, and facts: 'Objects form the substance of the world' (TLP 2.021). He also holds a picture theory of meaning where the structure of language (or thought) is isomorphic with the structure of the states of affairs that the language pictures. Language thus 'pictures' reality, but importantly, there are limits to language in terms of what it can picture and 'what we cannot speak about we must pass over in silence' (TLP 7).

However, by the *PI*, Wittgenstein rejects the view that the 'world has one fixed logical structure, or, alternatively, that propositions have one fixed logical structure' (Putnam 2008: 7) and rejects the picture theory of meaning and the 'Augustinian' view of language where 'words in language name objects' (PI 1). This is a rejection of a correspondence or referential view of meaning, wherein words directly refer to, or 'pick out', entities in the world. Wittgenstein argues that this view must be false as there are words in our language that simply cannot be accounted for on a representationalist account.

Instead, Wittgenstein argues in favour of a use theory of meaning: 'For a large class of cases of the employment of the word "meaning" – though not for all – this word can be explained in this way: the meaning of a word is its use in the language' (PI 43). Under this account, there is nothing more that we can do to understand the meaning of a word than to describe how it is used by speakers of the language in which the word appears.

Strongly related to Wittgenstein's meaning-as-use claim is his discussion of 'language-games'. Rejecting the possibility of private languages, Wittgenstein argues that the meanings of terms are constrained and shaped by the languagegame in which they appear. Very roughly, a language-game is a set of rules and meanings that have been accepted by some community of speakers, relative to the sorts of information that those speakers need to convey and communicate, as well as the broader 'form of life' that the language-game reflects. Language is thus an activity, and a language cannot be understood or interpreted independent of that activity (PI 23).

For example, in one language-game, a word might be used to refer to an object, but, in another language-game, that same word might be used to ask a question or give an order. 'Water', to use one of Wittgenstein's own examples, might vary in this way. In one language-game, it simply refers to water; in another, it is a demand that someone bring someone some water. The meaning of the word varies depending on the language-game in which it is uttered.

All of this, if correct, leaves the realist in a very difficult position. First, if words are not taken to 'pick out' objects in the world, then in what sense can we maintain that we have any ability to accurately use those words to describe mind-independent reality? Second, the realist tries to use language to speak 'objectively' about the world. That is, the realist tries to provide the 'God's-Eye view' on the world. However, if words are tied to the language-game in which they appear, there is no sense in which we can arrive at an 'objective' meaning for those words. There is no 'God's-Eye view'; only views from within a language-game and the associated forms of life.

Wittgenstein's views about language therefore place the sorts of claims that realists want to maintain as true and meaningful, as being beyond the limits of our language. The realist, and the metaphysician more broadly, tries to use language for a purpose that it simply cannot fulfil. Note Wittgenstein is *not* arguing that there is no mind-independent reality. This is because to even try to make the claim that mind-independent entities exist or not is to try to speak about something that cannot be spoken about. The mistake that the realist makes is to be tricked by language. Language appears to allow us to speak about the mind-independent world, but the realist is, in fact, speaking only nonsense.

Carnap: Linguistic Frameworks and the Internal/External Distinction

In the past fifteen years, arguably there has been no one that has been more influential in the realism debate than Rudolf Carnap, in part due to the growing interest in the domain of metametaphysics and a 'rediscovery' of interest in his work (see, inter alia, Blatti and Lapointe 2016; Carus 2007; Friedman and Creath 2007; Pincock 2009; Price 2009; Uebel 2018). Amongst many others that could have been chosen, here are two quotes that summarise Carnap's overall views on metaphysics:

> This term [metaphysics] is used in this paper, as usually in Europe, for the field of alleged knowledge of the essence of things which transcends the realm of empirically founded, inductive science.
>
> (1932; reprinted 1959: Notes to section 1)

> The metaphysicians wish to seek their object behind the objects of empirical science; they wish to enquire after the essence – the ultimate cause of things. But the logical analysis of the pretended propositions of metaphysics has shown that they are not propositions at all but empty word arrays, which on

account of notional and emotional connections arouse the false appearance of being propositions. (Carnap 1934: 5)

Much of Carnap's output, particularly in his later years, focuses on fairly technical issues within the philosophy of science, semantics, and inductive logic. And although there are anti-metaphysical and anti-realist, elements throughout Carnap's work (especially in Carnap 1932/1959; see also Kraut 2020), I will limit the discussion here to (in my view) his most important and influential anti-realist argument, found most clearly stated 'Empiricism, Semantics and Ontology' (1950).

At least since Quine (1948), questions that ask whether some entity exists are meant to be the central question of ontology, itself taken to be a central part of metaphysics. The 'what exists?' question is taken to be a substantive question to ask and one that, at least in principle, is possible to answer the question with respect to the mind-independent world. The 'ontologist' is thus conceived as a realist – they believe that there exists a mind-independent reality and that by answering the 'what exists?' question, we arrive at true claims about the nature of that mind-independent reality.

In 'Empiricism, Semantics, and Ontology', Carnap argues that asking the 'what exists?' question cannot provide substantive metaphysical answers. Instead, claims about the existence of a given entity (or set of entities) cannot be not revealing of the nature of reality, and answers to the 'what exists?' question will be trivially (or analytically) true (or false) due to the nature of language rather than due to the way that the world itself is.

First, Carnap introduces the notion of a linguistic framework. A linguistic framework is a set of rules and 'ways of speaking': systems that are introduced to talk about a particular set of entities. Frameworks allow us to talk about entities that are relevant to the purpose of that framework. Ordinary language, for example, is a mixture of linguistic frameworks. In different situations, we jump between those frameworks depending on the conversational need at the time. But some frameworks will be more specific and specialised. For example, a mathematical linguistic framework – a language created to do mathematics – has been specifically created to allow us to talk about things like numbers and investigate what numbers are like.

Carnap's central claim is that the meaning of words differs from framework to framework and that the question of what the meaning of any term is cannot be given any sense outside of a framework. Asking what the term 'number' means, without specifying the framework it is used within, is to try to strip away the context that contributes to the word's meaning. For Carnap, we could not even begin to say what 'number' means within first being told about the language framework that the word is part of as the very meaning of the term is itself dependent upon the wider language framework that it is part of. A word outside of a linguistic framework is meaningless.

Such a claim might seem innocent to a realist at first. The realist might think that it is fine that a term like 'number' changes its meaning from one framework to the next. However, Carnap does not limit this variation to words like 'number' and instead argues that all terms, including crucial notions for the realist like 'truth' and 'exists' are also framework-relative (though cf. Thomasson 2015: section 1). It is this that is highly damaging to the realist position. The realist wants to be able to speak about the objective nature of mind-independent reality. The realist wants to be able to ask (and answer) questions about what *really* exists. The realist wants to ask not merely whether numbers exist within the mathematical linguistic framework but whether numbers exist independently of any linguistic framework and independently of language at all. For Carnap, such questions that purport to stand outside of any linguistic framework are meaningless.

To be clear, Carnap does not deny that we can meaningfully ask any ontological questions. However, such questions are only meaningful when asked *within* a framework. Carrying on with our example, within a mathematical framework, we can ask the ontological question of 'do numbers exist?' and presumably answer 'yes'. Numbers, we can therefore conclude, do exist, but this answer only reveals something about the linguistic framework that the question was asked within. Indeed, in many cases, it will simply be trivially or analytically true, as the existence of numbers is implied by the relevant linguistic framework. Therefore, answering the question 'do numbers exist?' positively within the mathematical linguistic framework only tells us that numbers exist *within that framework*. No further conclusions can be drawn from this, and in other frameworks it might be false that numbers exist.

Carnap calls these meaningful ontological questions asked within a framework 'internal questions'. These are contrasted with 'external questions'. External questions are those that the realist is trying to ask and answer. They are an attempt to ask whether some entity exists *independent* of a linguistic framework. As the word 'exists' (as well as all other words) has no meaning outside of the framework, such questions simply make no sense. To ask them, or to try to answer them, is to simply speak nonsense. When the realist tries to make claims about the existence or nature of entities outside of a linguistic framework, those statements are meaningless or empty of content.

The only external question that Carnap allows that we can legitimately ask – the only question that stands apart from a particular linguistic framework – is to ask which framework we should adopt. However, the answer to this is not metaphysical; it is pragmatic, depending upon the needs and intentions of the speaker. Thus, we could ask whether I should adopt the mathematical linguistic framework when I am trying to buy a coffee. Presumably, in that situation, doing so would be pragmatically bad. But this pragmatic choice of language is not enough to save realism.

If Carnap is right, to accept the reality of the 'thing world' (as Carnap characterises the metaphysical realist) is only to accept a certain form of language and accept the rules that lead to a language of that form. The reality of the thing world cannot be among such statements within a language – such a statement cannot be formulated within a language, as the limit of the language is only the ontological commitments that come from the set of rules that govern that language. We might initially think that the success of the thing language provides a reason for thinking that the thinglanguage has some claim to being correct (or true). But Carnap notes that this would only support the pragmatic decision to accept the thing language over other languages that are less pragmatically useful to our needs – something far short of the justification that the realist needs to support their claims. Differing linguistic frameworks cannot be said to be 'better' or 'worse' than each other, at least not with respect to some objective criteria or their ability to describe mind-independent reality. Rather, frameworks are only 'better' or 'worse' relative to the purposes for which they are introduced. When we are doing mathematics, the mathematical linguistic framework is likely the best, pragmatically, to adopt; when doing biology, the biological linguistic framework is likely the best, pragmatically, to adopt; etc. (though cf. Miller 2021). To try to do metaphysics, or to be a realist, is to mistakenly think that illegitimate external questions can be both validly asked and answered.

It might be tempting here to think of Carnap as endorsing some pluralist but still realist account of metaphysics. The different linguistic frameworks perform different jobs, and so we might initially be led into thinking that Carnap was pluralistic about which entities exist. However, this would be incorrect (see Price 2009: 324–5). The position rather is pluralistic about *language*, and from that pluralism, Carnap draws his critique of realism. If we have many different linguistic frameworks, all of which have their own supposed ontological commitments, then, as choosing between those frameworks is an external question, we have no basis for that choice beyond pragmatic benefit in a given situation. As Ney puts it, Carnap's anti-realism is thus based on the claim that 'metaphysicians distort language in various ways to produce statements that in the end prove meaningless' (2012: 55). Or, in Carnap's own words: 'the possibility of forming pseudo-statements [i.e., realist statements] is based on a logical defect in language' (1932/1959: 69).

Dummett: Justificationism, Bivalence, and Indefinite Extensibility

Throughout his career, Dummett proposed various arguments relating to realism and anti-realism. Here, I will highlight just a few aspects – see Green (2001) for a more detailed overview of Dummett's work on language and its relation to realism.

Dummett closely ties the outcome of the realism debate to issues concerning meaning, holding that, for any given debate, it will only be possible to conclude in favour of the realist or anti-realist once a suitable theory of meaning has been worked out. For this reason, Dummett is not a 'global anti-realist', even at one point suggesting that the view might be incoherent (1978: 367). However, on metaphysical realism, Dummett does come down on the side of the anti-realist.

To see why, we need to consider the realist's theory of meaning. Realism, for Dummett, involves the acceptance of a truth-conditional theory of meaning which holds that a sentence is true iff the truth-conditions expressed by that sentence are satisfied. The realist endorses this theory as it provides a link between the mind-independent world and our language. However, Dummett argues that there is no evidence in our use of language that shows that we can make any such link, and truth-conditional accounts leave upon the possibility that there are cases under which we may never know if the conditions are satisfied or not. Or, put another way, the realist's posited link between our words and the world does not manifest (hence why this is sometimes known as the 'manifestation' argument; see Dummett 1978, 1993; Tennant 1987; Wright 1993).

Dummett instead defends a 'justificationist' semantics under which 'the meaning, or the content, is given by what we count as justifying an assertion of the statement, or an assertion whose content is that of the thought' (2005: 673). Truth is also explained in terms of justification: 'a statement to be true only if there exists something that would justify its assertion, and similarly for the truth of a thought' (2005: 673). This provides a quite general argument for anti-realism, even if it is not an argument for global anti-realism. A justificationist semantics means that linguistic understanding must always be connected to how the word is used in practice (note the similarity to the Wittgensteinian idea of meaning as use), and the meaning of words must be communicable (see Dummett 1978: 420–31). Realism is guilty of trying to endorse the truth of sentences that cannot be justified and hence of breaking that connection between meaning and use.

Importantly, justificationist semantics leads to a form of anti-realism, but not solipsism or idealism: 'What is justificationism? The justificationist is not a solipsist, or even a phenomenalist: he does not think that reality-all that exists consists solely of our experience . . . . The justificationist thus accepts that there is an external world, an environment common to himself and other human beings and to other animals, too' (Dummett 2005: 672).

What is missing for the realist is the ability to know or speak meaningfully about the nature of the mind-independent world.

For Dummett, then, the difference between realism and anti-realism is, in part, a matter of which theory of meaning is accepted. This is only 'in part' as Dummett also argues that debates about realism are disputes over logic, holding that the realism debate significantly concerns whether we accept the principle of bivalence. The principle of bivalence holds that every proposition is determinately either true or false. Dummett argues that while the realist is committed to accepting the principle of bivalence, the justificationist must reject it as if there is nothing that can justify whether a statement is true or false, it cannot be true or false. This is not merely a point about whether we *know* whether the statement is true or false. Due to the nature of truth within justificationist semantics, certain statements will be neither true nor false, irrespective of our knowledge of this (see Dummett 2005: 673).

Again here, Dummett is arguing that the realism debate is not really about what it appeared at first to be about. It is not about the existence or independence of reality. Rather, it is a debate about meaning or logic. Given this, the natural line of response for the realist on these issues will be to deny Dummett's views about meaning, his claims about the principle of bivalence being a core commitment of realism, or the importance of a realist notion of truth for various purposes, including for science. For more discussion of these sorts of responses, see Edgington (1981), Hellman (1989, 1992), Pagin (1988), Khlentzos (2021), and Sandqvist (2009).

A last major influence of Dummett's work on the realism debate can be found in his work on indefinite extensibility. This argument attempts to problematise the notion of 'object' that is required by the realist. The central idea is that the realist needs a concept of 'object' that can extend over every object, whatever its nature or kind. In the Quinean tradition, this is sometimes phrased as the realist holding that quantification is unrestricted. The realist needs such a notion to ensure that when they use the term 'object', they truly are using it to refer to every *thing* and not just some subset of things. However, indefinite extensibility seems to undermine this notion of 'object'.

The seeds of this argument can be found in Russell's discussion of the set paradoxes (see Russell 1907, 1908) but were brought to the fore by Dummett who defines 'indefinitely extensible' as: ' A concept is indefinitely extensible if, for any definite characterization of it, there is a natural extension of this characterization, which yields a more inclusive concept; this extension will be made according to some general principle for generating such extensions, and, typically, the extended characterization will be formulated by reference to the previous, unextended, characterization' (Dummett 1963: 195–6; see also Linnebo 2018).

In other words, the problem is that any attempt to draw a limit to the extension of 'object' will fail, for there will be some other extension that is larger and that this process with repeat indefinitely. Just as Russell's paradox raised problems about the set of all sets, there seemingly cannot be an all-inclusive concept of 'object' for the realist to rely on. There is no way to talk about all 'objects' as the notion of 'object' is indefinitely extensible, and the meaning of 'object' will always be relative to the conceptual scheme in which it appears.

The realist might respond that they do not need such an unrestricted concept of 'object', but any such move then seems to run into the related problem of which of the now restricted notions of 'object' is the privileged one (a position closely related to the realist but metaphysically deflationary position developed by Thomasson (2009, 2015) and Hirsch 2011). The realist has a problem in showing which restriction on the meaning of 'object' is 'better', metaphysically speaking. Going down this route, there is a danger that the problems of conceptual relativity will reimpose themselves.

There is a lot more that could be said about unrestricted quantification and whether it is possible or not. For those interested, a good place to start is Fine (2006) or Dorr (2005). See also Williamson (2003), Florio (2014), Rayo (2020), Warren (2017a), and Miller (2014: section 3.3).

3.3.2 Ideal Theories, the Model-Theoretic Argument, and Conceptual Relativity: Putnam

It is hard to overstate Hilary Putnam's influence on the realism debate. Putnam both develops further lines of arguments found in earlier rejections of realism and entirely novel critiques of realism. Even the modern-day conception of realism owes much to Putnam (cf. Sections 2.3 and 2.4). Indeed, so influential is Putnam that we have already discussed his important 'brain-in-a-vat' arguments against realism in Section 3.1, and there is still a need for this section devoted solely to (some of) his other arguments. Even with this section, a full outline and discussion of Putnam would require more than I have the space to do here. What follows will be an outline highlighting certain key aspects of Putnam's work. My readings will draw heavily on Button's (2013) remarkably clear exposition and discussion of Putnam's views – those interested in the technical details and more advanced discussion of Putnam's arguments, especially the model-theoretic arguments, are advised to look there.

Externalist and Internalist Perspectives

In *Reason, Truth and History*, Putnam outlines the 'externalist' view that he argues against. The externalist perspective holds that 'The world consists of some fixed totality of mind-independent objects. There is exactly one true and complete description of 'the way the world is'. Truth involves some sort of correspondence relation between words or thought-signs and external things and sets of things' (1981: 49).

Button (2013: 7–11) characterises this as the acceptance of three principles:

> The Independence Principle: The world is (largely) made up of objects that are mind-, language-, and theory-independent.

> The Correspondence Principle: Truth involves some sort of correspondence relation between words or thought-signs and external things and sets of things.

> The Cartesianism Principle: Even an entirely ideal theory might be radically false.

The opposing position, Putnam says, 'has no unambiguous name' (1981: 49) but he classifies his preferred position as the internalist perspective, which consists of three (parallel) claims:

> 'Objects' do not exist independently of conceptual schemes. (1981: 52)

> Asking what objects exist 'only makes sense . . . within a theory or description'. (1981: 49)

> Truth . . . is some sort of (idealized) rational acceptability, [an] ideal coherence of our beliefs with each other and with our experiences as those experiences are themselves represented in our belief system. (1981: 49–50)

The externalist perspective is what we have simply been calling realism – the independence principle aligns to a combination of what I called existence and independence (Section 2.2), and the correspondence principle was discussed, albeit in different terms, in Section 2.3. The Cartesianism principle is connected to the uniqueness claims discussed in Section 2.4, as well as the realist's commitment to the correspondence theory of truth: if truth is correspondence, then truth is non-epistemic, and hence however useful the truths that we currently accept are, they might all turn out to be so mistaken. The internalist perspective is Putnam's anti-realist alternative, though Putnam himself characterised his view as a form of realism, just not 'metaphysical' realism but 'Internal Realism', which I will return to towards the end of this section.

Model-Theoretic Argument(s)

Putnam's model-theoretic argument – or better arguments for there are several related arguments – targets the first and second externalist claims. There is not the space to cover all the model-theoretic arguments in this Element, and some make use of various technical aspects that would also be better covered by the work more specifically devoted to these arguments. Here, I will (attempt) a non-technical summary of *some* of Putnam's model-theoretic arguments, leaving technical aspects aside where possible.

Following Button (2013: section 2), we can distinguish two families of model-theoretic arguments. The first are indeterminacy arguments. These seek to show that if a theory can be made true, then there will be multiple ways in which it could be made true contradicting the realist commitment to there being only one true and complete description of the way the world is. The second are infallibilism arguments that hold that every ideal theory can be made true, directly opposing the Cartesianism principle that even an ideal theory might be false. Together, Putnam's model-theoretic arguments will lead to a problem for the realist in explaining how it is that our words or concepts can be accurately 'mapped' onto the world. The realist will be left with no way in which we can specify what the reference relation between our words and the world amounts to.

Let us start with (one of) the indeterminacy arguments. Suppose that a realist has some theory, T. T is a theory about the nature of the mind-independent world, and let us also suppose that T is true in the sense that it is possible to map the terms that appear within T onto the entities within the world. T contains various terms. These can be thought of as labels (or names) for the entities in the world. By hypothesis, for every entity in the world, T contains some term for that entity, as well as terms for any collections of entities.

Imagine that we now shuffle the entities around while leaving the terms in place within the theory. The same sentences will be true before and after the shuffling. This is because, while the labels may have moved, the models that we have before and after the shuffling have a distinct but isomorphic structure. All we have done is move the *labels*, leaving the structure of the initial mapping in place. Button calls this the 'permutation theorem': 'Any theory with a non-trivial model has many distinct isomorphic models with the same domain' (2013: 15).

The problem facing the realist is that we cannot decide between these models. The same sentences are true in each, and hence we have no clear way to specify the *intended* correspondence relation. By 'intended', we mean the correspondence relation that allows the realist to maintain the correspondence principle.

There are multiple different possible 'mappings' of the terms to the entities in the world, and all of those mappings can be shown to maintain the truth of sentences in T. The realist, for Putnam, cannot therefore determine which correspondence relation holding between our words and entities in the world is the 'correct' one. There is an indeterminacy of correspondence (or reference), undermining the correspondence principle. As Putnam puts it: 'It follows that there are always infinitely many different interpretations of the predicates of a language which assign the 'correct' truth-values to the sentences in all possible worlds, no matter how these 'correct' truth-values are singled out' (Putnam 1981: 35).

This is clearly a very bad conclusion for the realist. But, according to Putnam, it gets worse. Suppose that the theory T is 'ideal'. An ideal theory is one that satisfies all 'operational and theoretical constraints' (Putnam 1977: 494). According to the Cartesianism principle, due to the realists' commitment to a correspondence theory of truth, such an ideal theory should be such that it could still be false:

> The most important consequence of metaphysical realism is that truth is supposed to be radically non-epistemic – we might be 'brains in a vat' and so the theory that is 'ideal' from the view of operational utility, inner beauty and elegance, 'plausibility', simplicity, 'conservatism', etc., might be false. Verified (in any operational sense) does not imply 'true', on the metaphysical realist picture. (Putam 1978: 125)

However, Putnam's infallibility arguments aim to show that an ideal theory cannot be false, contra the Cartesianism principle.

The argument for this is fairly simple. Borrowing the outline from Button (2013: 17), if a theory is ideal, then it will, presumably, be consistent. This is because consistency is a theoretical virtue that we normally care about and hence will be a feature of an ideal theory, and because inconsistent theories can be shown, within classical systems, to entail everything. By the completeness theorem, any consistent theory will have a model that makes it true. That is, there will be some model of the theory that has the same cardinality of the world such that we can map one-to-one between the individuals in the model to the entities in the world. Therefore, if the theory is ideal, there is guaranteed to be a way to make it true. The realist therefore cannot maintain that an ideal theory might be false.

We have seen two model-theoretic problems for the realist. First, they cannot say which of the interpretations of a theory is the intended one, and second, even the ideal theory might be false. One way the realist might respond is by finding some way to fix the correspondence between our terms and the world. For example, the realist might appeal to some causal relation holding between terms and entities. Or the realist might introduce distinctions between those entities that are 'elite' or 'natural' (see Lewis 1984) and those that are not.

Button (2013: section 3) provides some arguments against these specific forms of response. However, as he also notes, such attempts to fix correspondence and counter-arguments are always going to be piecemeal in nature. It would lead to an almost endless back and forth between the realist and their opponents. To genuinely prove that realism is flawed, Putnam needs to show that whatever the realist might posit to fix correspondence – or to determine what is the *intended* interpretation amongst the *unintended* ones – it will fail. Putnam argues that just such a general argument can be given through his 'just-more-theory manoeuvre'.

Take the causal restraint already mentioned. Roughly, the idea would be that the realist can say that the intended interpretation is the one wherein there are the appropriate causal relations holding between our terms and the world. These causal relations distinguish the intended interpretation from the unintended ones. However, Putnam argues that if the realist posits this causal connection, then it is an addition to the ideal theory. That is, the causal claim is 'just-more' – just another posit – of the theory. Once we recognise it as being just-more-theory, the anti-realist can simply run the model-theoretic argument(s) again. There will, once again, be different interpretations that will assign different extensions to the terms of the theory, and this will now include differing extensions for the new terms the realist response added. And, assuming that the theory that contains this new addition is consistent, there will again be a model on which the theory comes out as true (see Elgin 1995). There is no addition that we could make that would block this reapplication of the initial arguments, and no way for the realist to maintain the ideal theory could be false or to 'fix' correspondence. As Button puts it: 'Putnam treats any statement of an additional interpretative constraint as just more theory: more grist for his model-theoretic mill' (2013: 29).

How can the realist respond? Most have focused on the just-more-theory manoeuvre as the weak link. For example, Devitt (1983), Lewis (1984), and Wright and Hale (2017) have argued that the argument is question begging. The idea, roughly, is that Putnam's just-more-theory manoeuvre does not suitably recognise the role of the additional constraints that the realist posits. If correct, this would mean that there is some additional constraint that enables the realist to specify what is the 'correct' correspondence relation.

It is worth noting, though, that often what is posited as the additional constraint by realists are primitive posits, such as Lewis' posit of 'naturalness'. For Lewis, there is a gradation of more or less 'natural' properties (Lewis 1984: 227–8), which the more natural properties carving the world closer to its joints. The correct model then is the one wherein the predicates of the model only refer to perfectly natural properties. Perfectly natural properties are 'reference magnets' (Lewis 1983, 1984).

Of course, positing this gradation of more or less natural properties to resolve the model-theoretical arguments incurs a metaphysical cost. And whether we think any primitive-invoking response is successful will depend on whether we are willing to accept that posit, or any other primitive notion that we might try to employ. It is possible that only those antecedently disposed towards realism will find such approaches entirely satisfying.

Conceptual Relativity

In *The Many faces of Realism* (1987), Putnam puts forward a different argument against realism by attempting to undermine the dichotomy between the external and the internal that the realist wishes to maintain. In this, Putnam sees himself as taking Kant as his inspiration – 'as a forefather, not . . . as scripture' (1987: 43), as Kant is 'not committed to, but rather suggests a rejection of, the distinction between things in themselves and projections' (1987: 43).

Putnam's arguments in this work amount to a denial that there is a point where we can delineate between the subjective and the objective – that there is no way in which we can make a principled decision about whether a predication in language relates to a real property or merely a reflection of our culture or interests. The lack of a methodologically satisfactory way to make this cut is exhibited for Putnam through the philosophical disagreements that we see. For example (and following Putnam's example), the position upon the subjective/ objective scale that philosophers place counterfactual statements varies hugely, some taking them to be an insight into objective matters about the world, others as only a subjective view we could take. Putnam suggests that we should simply reject this scale by rejecting the notion of objectivity entirely. Instead, echoing Carnap (cf. Section 3.3.1), objectivity is only relative to a conceptual scheme:

> *Given* a language, we can describe the 'facts' that make a sentence of that language true and false in a 'trivial' way – using the sentences of that very language; but the dream of finding a well-defined Universal Relation between a (supposed) totality of *all* facts and an arbitrary true sentence in an arbitrary language, is just the dream of an absolute notion of fact . . . and of an absolute relation between sentences and the facts . . . 'in themselves'; the very dream whose hopelessness I hoped to expose. (Putnam 1987: 40)

This does not force Putnam into some form of ontological relativity. Putnam, as Carnap before, denies the thesis that there is no notion of a 'better' or 'worse' conceptual scheme. The conceptual scheme 'restricts the "space" of descriptions available to us; but it does not predetermine the answers to our questions' (1987: 39). Note that this also echoes Goodman, who stresses that the '[w]illingness to accept countless alternative true or right world-versions does not mean that everything goes . . . , but only that truth must be otherwise conceived than as correspondence with a ready-made world' (Goodman 1978: 94).

Once the objective/subjective scale is relative to a language or conceptual scheme, realism loses its ability to maintain that it can describe mind-independent reality. Terms that the realist might try to use, such as 'fact', 'exist', and 'object', cannot be used independently from a conceptual scheme. The realist's uses of the terms 'objective' or 'external' are meaningless.

For Putnam, the ontological commitments that we should accept are simply those that the language or theory that we have accepted demands of us. If a theory requires abstract entities, for example, then we should accept abstract entities into our ontology. Granted that we have no universally accepted theory or language, there is also therefore no universally accepted ontology: 'we don't have a single, unified theory of the world off of which to read our ontology' (Putnam 2004: 81). This is known as the argument from conceptual relativity. Realism is shown to be false as it cannot secure the 'objective' grounding that it needs. Putnam's work on conceptual relativity has been highly influential inside and outside of the realism debate. Here are two examples relevant to realism and anti-realism.

A first influence is on Hirsch's 'Quantifier Variance Thesis'. The quantifier variance thesis focuses on the variability of the meaning of the term 'exists' in different languages. Hirsch uses this to 'deflate' metaphysics, arguing that metaphysical disputes are 'merely verbal', with those debates being actually about what version of 'exists' (or of the existential quantifier) we should use (Hirsch 2011). Hirsch's work has been discussed extensively in the metametaphysical literature, so I will not try to rehearse arguments for or against it here. For those interested, good places to start are Sud and Manley (2020) and Hirsch and Warren (2019).

Interestingly, Hirsch takes his view to be consistent with realism (Hirsch 2002). This is because Hirsch characterises realism as solely being the combination of existence and independence. Eklund (2008) interprets this to mean that Hirsch accepts that the world is an amorphous lump, though Miller (2016) has argued that even if this is the correct interpretation, then it is not enough to make Hirsch's position count as 'realist'. Naturally, who is right here will depend on what commitments outlined in Section 2 we take to be constitutive of realism.

Another view influenced by Putnam's work on conceptual relativity (and by Dummett's related work; see Dummett 1981) is conventionalism.

Conventionalism holds that the way in which we conceptualise the world is merely a reflection of us and the ways that we happen to think. How we view the world and hence what we think exists and the nature of those existents are inescapably conventional and cannot be taken to be reflective of the mind-independent world itself.

Putting this in a slightly different way, the realist typically holds that the world contains real mind-independent boundaries or distinctions. This can be derived from the realist's commitment to existence and independence, and the realist is committed to accessibility in that 'joints in reality are supposed to act as the basis of our efforts to classify reality, and common sense suggests that most of these attempts are successful' (Tahko 2012: 405). As noted before, the realist need not think *all* boundaries are mind-independent. Indeed, most people are likely to think some boundaries are objective and others are subjective. To be a realist, it is enough to think that there are some mind-independent boundaries in nature and that we can (at least in principle) come to discover them. To oppose realism then is to endorse the view that there is no way to know which of our concepts are merely conventional and which carve nature at its joints, or that 'all our efforts to determine natural boundaries are subjective' (Tahko 2012: 406).

Why might we think that all boundaries are 'the product of some cognitive or social fiat' (Varzi 2011: 142; see also Smith and Varzi 2000)? Often, conventionalism is arrived at via a progression. First, we can recognise that various seemingly 'real' boundaries that we perceive in the world are merely subjective or are the product of cognitive or social fiats. For example, the boundaries between countries are recognised to be social. Then, the boundaries of rivers, mountains, and other intuitive more 'natural' entities can be doubted. After all, where, precisely, does Mount Everest start and end? And so on, for all boundaries we might perceive in the world.

The immediate realist response is to accept that some of these boundaries are subjective or mind-dependent in some way but try to hold that at some point in our understanding of the world, objective boundaries become apparent. However, even in physics, there are multiple different ways of classifying elements and other types of entities. Thus, by slow progression, the conventionalist makes the case that all classification is subjective or mind-dependent.

Conventionalists also often point to claims about composition to further their case:

> Consider the debate on unrestricted composition. There is no question that we feel more at ease with certain mereological composites than with others. We feel at ease, for instance, with regard to such things as the fusion of Tibbles's

parts (whatever they are), or even a platypus's parts; but when it comes to such unlovely and gerrymandered mixtures as trout-turkeys, consisting of the front half of a trout and the back half of a turkey, we feel uncomfortable. Such feelings may exhibit surprising regularities across contexts and cultures. Yet, arguably they rest on psychological biases and *Gestalt* factors that needn't have any bearing on how the world is actually structured. (Varzi 2011: 144–5)

For the conventionalist, the reason that we favour some classifications over others is simply psychological bias. Amongst the various options available, either in terms of classifying entities or deciding when it is the case that composition has occurred, there are multiple different ways in which we could carve up the world. Indeed, the problem is that there are too many differences that we could draw upon to classify the world, and there is no non-subjective way to choose one classification scheme over any other. As with Putnam's own conceptual relativity, conventionalism therefore builds an argument for the view that there are multiple different ways to describe the world and that there is no good way to prove or show that any one of them is 'better' with respect to accurately describing mind-independent reality.

It is important, though, to see that the conventionalist needs both claims. The realist can happily accept that there are multiple different classification schemes. What is needed for anti-realism is the additional claim that no classification can be shown to provide a 'privileged' description of reality. This is a weak point in the argument that some realists have focused on. That is, the most common realist response is to argue that there is some description or classification that is better than the others with respect to describing the world. Or, at least, that there could be such a classification. Debates on this topic tend to focus on specific cases, arguing for or against conventionalism with respect to a particular sort or type of entity, for example, Sidelle (1992) on identity claims and Heller (2008) on persistence. More general discussions can be found in Sosa (1999), Tahko (2012), and Varzi (2014).

Anti-realism and 'Internal Realism'

The idea that the facts admit of more than one picture has been around for over a century, however. It is anticipated by Herz's talk of equally good 'world pictures' in the introduction to his Principles of Mechanics, and it is referred to by William James.

(Putnam 1992b: 110)

Putnam, unlike some other anti-realists, sees himself as having taken a 'long journey from realism back to realism ... but not ... back to the metaphysical version of realism' (1999: 49). Putnam's 'realism' is based on an acceptance that the truth of a statement depends in part on the world beyond the speaker.

He is therefore not denying existence or independence. However, Putnam (following and crediting William James who is also a major influence of Putnam's wider commitment to pragmatism) stresses the need to preserve 'the insight that "description" is never a mere copying and that we constantly add to the ways in which language can be responsible to reality' (1999: 9).

The mistake of realism comes from 'supposing that the term reality must refer to a single superthing' (1999: 9). For the realist, this 'superthing' limits or structures all the possible thoughts that we can have and fixes the totality of possible knowledge claims independently of language users themselves. But Putnam holds that it is only a contingent fact about finite human abilities that limits the number of conceptual schemes that can be created. Knowledge claims only need to be coherent within the conceptual scheme that they are designed to apply within, and hence there is no need for any 'external reality' or 'way things-are-in-themselves' that limit possible knowledge claims. The realist is mistaken because the needed separation of metaphysical claims from language and concepts is impossible. Without some identifiable privileged access to the world, the realist is, for Putnam, not only incorrect, but the very notions that they wish to discuss the mind-independent and 'unconceptualised' reality, are taken by Putnam to be indescribable and unfit for any purpose (Mueller and Fine 2005).

Of course, even under this picture, we can create an ontology: a list of the entities that a given theory or language takes to exist, but this is as far as ontology can go. Take our everyday perception of the world as an example to illustrate this. It contains various macroscopic entities such as chairs and tables. For Putnam, this is a particular ontological view of the world and one which is supported by the ontological commitments that can be derived from our everyday language. Our everyday language allows for chairs to exist, but not mereological compositions of a chair and the Eiffel Tower. This language (and the related conceptual scheme) furnishes us with an ontology.

This ontology may be correct in the sense of being the one that arises from our ordinary language. But it can make no claim to be the *sole* correct description of the world, as this would be to adopt the notions of a mind-independent, unconceptualised reality. The claim that a posited ontology hooks up with the world – with some deeper, mind-independent structure of the world – is unjustifiable under Putnam's proposals. To provide an ontology is to simply read our commitments off the chosen language or conceptual scheme. This recognition that we can still provide an ontology is why Putnam views himself as a realist, albeit not one about 'external' realist. His realism is 'internal' to a conceptual scheme, and hence, Putnam labels his view 'Internal Realism'.

4 The Prospects for Realism

Metaphysical realism was initially summarised as the view that there exists some mind-independent entity (or entities). We then further clarified that for many, realism carries with it additional commitments, such as accessibility or uniqueness. This means that even if we are to accept metaphysical realism, there are a multitude of further more fine-grained realist debates to be had. For example, if we accept that there are mind-independent entities, are those entities properties? Are they objects? Are they processes? Are causes mind-independent, and what about laws of nature? The ontological commitments of views that would be classified as realist on the account given here will vary widely, and some views will be less ontologically committed than others.

Accepting a less ontologically committed form of realism might provide some defence against certain anti-realist arguments. This is because we could accept specific forms of anti-realism for certain troublesome sorts or kinds of entities while still maintaining a metaphysically realist view in the broader sense. Perhaps, for example, we think that there are good arguments against realism about laws of nature. We might have good reasons to think that laws of nature are not part of the mind-independent world. Such a view is, of course, perfectly consistent with accepting realism about some other sort of entity. Thus, we could start with the default view of realism about all entities, and then retreat, where needed, to anti-realism on a case-by-case basis. After this process, whatever we are left with, we accept. This would lead to being ontologically committed to fewer entities than some others might be, but so long as some entity/entities were left, we would still be able to accept metaphysical realism as outlined in this Element.

Such an approach, though, will not provide a defence against most of the objections mentioned in this Element as those arguments do not tend to focus on just one sort of entity. That is, the objections we have seen previously do not discriminate. They apply whether we are trying to defend a realism that accepts only properties, or a realism that accepts objects and properties, or a realism that accepts events but not properties, and so on for other variations.

This may lead some to think that the picture is unpromising for realism. There are many objections, and while there are some responses, supporting realism might feel like being in a philosophical game of 'whack-a-mole' as we attempt to respond to every anti-realist argument that is developed. The realist seems less focused on putting forward arguments *for* realism than on developing arguments *against* anti-realism, idealism, or scepticism (or some other non-realist view). This way of defending realism is, as a consequence, quite piecemeal and reactionary, and heavily reliant on the (supposed) intuitiveness of realism as being the 'default' or 'common-sense' view.

There are, though, some trends in the ways that realists try to respond to the objections. One more general approach is to reject one or more of the commitments that have been problematised. For example, it has been suggested that accepting a correspondence theory of truth might be a requirement for the realist. But we might note that this is a requirement that Putnam – himself an anti-realist – imposes on the realist and one that Putnam then rejects as part of his arguments against realism. The realist might, somewhat fairly, complain that it is not up to the anti-realist to define realism, and if it turns out that realism does not require accepting correspondence, then automatically various arguments can be dismissed. Devitt (1983, 1991) and Millikan (1986) have taken this line; see also Cox (2003) who argues that realism is compatible with deflationary truth.

Other examples of this sort of approach are Smart's (1982) argument against Putnam that realists need to think that the ideal theory could be false by providing an example of a theory that would never be rational to accept but could be true; Smith's (2002) argument that the realism does not require there being one maximally adequate way of describing the world; and Miller's (2021) argument that we can provide a way to suitably compare languages to begin to arrive at a view as to which is metaphysically 'best' or 'privileged'. In each case, the realist is trying to show that realism is not committed to some problematic position or thesis – especially if that position or thesis is part of a definition of realism that was developed as part of an argument against realism.

Even if that approach is successful in some ways (and it is not clear that it always is), it is harder to see how it (or the insistence that realism is the 'default' view) helps with the epistemological problems facing realism. Throughout Section 3, we saw arguments that raised issues about how the realist can *know* that their claims are about the mind-independent world. How can we *know* that the entities are there, and how can we ever *know* about their nature? These epistemological concerns remain in need of an answer by realists too.

One way to provide an answer is to appeal to primitives. Thus, the realist wants to determine what is 'real' (rather than merely the real; see Fine 2001), or to find truths that can be stated using only terms that refer to 'perfectly natural' properties (Lewis 1984), or that are true in 'ontologese' (Sider 2011). Such primitive notions might help the realist by being reference-fixing devices or by allowing us to distinguish between occasions when we are aiming to talk about how the world *really* is, and when we are talking more loosely. But (somewhat understandably) if someone is not already antecedently committed to realism, appealing to these primitives is unlikely to be persuasive. For example, Putnam repeatedly calls attempts to fix reference in this way 'magic' (Putnam 1980: 101, 1981: 3–5, 46–8, 51; cf. Button 2013: chapter 4.3). To be clear, ideological and ontological primitives in our theories are unavoidable, so the concern is not merely that the realist has posited primitives. Rather, the concern is that the posited primitives are not warranted and/or do no explanatory work.

Some realists have taken up this challenge and tried to justify their primitives directly on the basis of their explanatory power. Sider, for instance, argues that we should accept his realist primitive notion 'structure' due to the explanatory power that doing so grants our theories. For Sider, theories that are 'based on bizarre, non-joint-carving classifications are unexplanatory even when true' (2011: 23). Sider also, more broadly, argues that certain notions are indispensable, again invoking the idea that theories without such posits have less explanatory power.

The core idea then is that we should be realists as being realists is fruitful. It leads to understanding, or at least understanding better, the world around us and can therefore be us justified on something like the grounds of inference to the best explanation (though see Allen 2002 for a critical discussion of inference to the best explanation defences of Lewis' notion of natural properties). This way of arguing for realism is therefore based on abductive reasoning. The realist argues that some entities of a particular sort or kind must exist on the basis of the explanatory power of the theory or because of some other theoretical virtue(s) the theory possesses such as simplicity or elegance, explanatory power, and so on (see Williamson 2016).

The problem, though, is, first, that it is not clear that the world itself must conform to theoretical virtues, and, second, it could be responded that the methods used by the realist – often a priori methods – are not reliable. That is, even if we accept in principle the use of abductive reasoning, why might we think that the best explanation of the phenomena, or the most explanatory theory, is the realist's theory. For arguments along these lines, see Benacerraf (1973) and Field (1988); see also Warren (2017b).

Arguing about explanatory power, appealing to abductive reasoning, or positing a primitive all pose a further risk for the realism debate as a whole: the risk of stalemate. On one side, there will be the realist who sees their position as the only sensible non-sceptical approach, and on the other side, anti-realists (or idealists, or sceptics, or those with some other anti-realist sentiments) who struggle to accept a view that seems to carry significant consequences on the basis of such claims or posits. Neither side is easily persuadable, and nor is it obvious what could significantly shift the needle for either realism or anti-realism. This would not be to hold that the debate between realists and anti-realists is merely verbal, but it is to suggest that it is not always clear what could provide a solution.

What then for the future of the realism debate? In my view, some hope to avoid stalemate comes from situating debates over realism within a wider metametaphysical context. It is already the case, as noted in Section 2.6, that there is an increasing recognition that the realism debate is part of the broader domain of metametaphysics and that one's position on the realism debate goes hand-in-hand with other commitments concerning the 'substantivity' of metaphysics.

If allowed a moment to speculate, I think that debates about realism will over time begin to take this metametaphysical element even more seriously, with defences of realism being combined with specific views about what metaphysics is and how it is to be done. Metaphysical realism as outlined here is a general thesis: one about the existence of some mind-independent reality. But we have repeatedly noted that there is a lingering epistemic issue as well: even if there is such a mind-independent world, can we access it? Realists are (largely) unified in responding 'yes' to this question but differ significantly about *how* it can be accessed. And this provides an example of how the broader metametaphysical discussion will be significant.

This is not the place to debate what metaphysics is (see Bliss and Miller 2020 for a wide scoping discussion on this), but what it is to be a realist will be very different if we think of metaphysics as being, for example, a solely a priori investigation into the world or if we think metaphysics should be 'naturalised'. These forms of realism will differ significantly not only in their epistemology of metaphysics – that is, on how it is that we can come to know about mind-independent entities – but also on whether or not they are susceptible to the sorts of criticisms raised by anti-realists. Various of the arguments raised in this Element against realism simply do not apply to some conceptions (though some apply more strongly too). Still, it suggests that what it means to be a realist will depend, to some degree, on what we take metaphysics itself to be.

Admittedly, this will likely complicate the debate and perhaps even make realism more parochial – to accept certain arguments for realism (or avoid certain anti-realist arguments), you will need to also accept at least some further metametaphysical claims. But it is not surprising that realism might need to be understood in the context of a wider metametaphysics. It is squarely in line with the increasing awareness that self-described metaphysicians (most of whom are realists) need to reflect more on the tools that they employ when doing metaphysics (e.g., Sider 2020).

It seems clear, to me at least, then that how we define metaphysics (a topic that could not be covered in detail in this Element) will be significant for the realism debate (and vice versa). And, this closer relationship between the realism debate and other metametaphysical issues can only aid in our attempts to further clarify (and possibly even in the future resolve) the realism debate. If stalemate can be avoided – and that is a big if – then this might be a promising route.

Bibliography

Adamson, P. 2015. *Philosophy in the Hellenistic and Roman Worlds*, New York: Oxford University Press.

Agada, A. 2019. 'Rethinking the Metaphysical Questions of Mind, Matter, Freedom, Determinism, Purpose and the Mind-Body Problem within the Panpsychist Framework of Consolationism', *South African Journal of Philosophy*, 38(1): 1–16.

Agada, A. 2021. *Consolationism and Comparative African Philosophy: Beyond Universalism and Particularism*, Oxford: Routledge.

Allen, S. 2002. 'Deepening the Controversy over Metaphysical Realism', *Philosophy*, 77(302): 519–41.

Allison, H. 2004. *Kant's Transcendental Idealism*, Revised and Enlarged ed., New Haven: Yale University Press.

Armstrong, D. M. 2004. *Truth and Truthmakers*, Cambridge: Cambridge University Press.

Asay, J. 2011. *Truthmaking, Truth and, Realism: New Work for a Theory of Truthmakers*. Doctoral thesis, University of North Carolina, Chapel Hill.

Asay, J. 2012. 'A Truthmaking Account of Realism and Anti-Realism', *Pacific Philosophical Quarterly*, 93(3): 373–94.

Ayer, A. J. 1952. *Language, Truth and Logic*, New York: Dover.

Benacerraf, P. 1973. 'Mathematical Truth', *Journal of Philosophy*, 70(19): 661–79.

Berkeley, G. 1948–1957. *The Works of George Berkeley, Bishop of Cloyne*, 9 vols., A. A. Luce and T. E. Jessop (eds.), London: Thomas Nelson.

Bigelow, J. 1988. *The Reality of Numbers: A Physicalist's Philosophy of Mathematics*, Oxford: Clarendon Press.

Bigelow, J. 2010. 'Quine, Mereology, and Inference to the Best Explanation', *Logique et Analyse*, 53(212): 465–82.

Blatti, S., and Lapointe, S. (eds.). 2016. *Ontology after Carnap*, Oxford: Oxford University Press.

Bliss, R., and Miller, J. T. M. (eds.). 2020. *The Routledge Handbook of Metametaphysics*, Oxford: Routledge.

Bradley, F. H. 1897. *Appearance and Reality*, London: Swan Sonnenschein; second edition.

Brueckner, A. L. 2010. *Essays on Skepticism*, Oxford: Oxford University Press.

Burnyeat, M. F. 1982. 'Idealism and Greek Philosophy: What Descartes Saw and Berkeley Missed', *The Philosophical Review*, 91(1): 3–40.

Button, T. 2013. *The Limits of Realism*, New York: Oxford University Press.

Carnap, R. 1932. 'Überwindung der Metaphysik durch logische Analyse der Sprache', *Erkenntnis*, 2: 219–41. Reprinted in 1959, 'Elimination of Metaphysics through Logical Analysis of Language', A. Pap (trans.), in A. J. Ayer (ed.), *Logical Positivism*, Glencoe: The Free Press, pp. 60–81.

Carnap, R. 1934. 'On the Character of Philosophic Problems', *Philosophy of Science*, 1(1): 5–19.

Carnap, R. 1950. 'Empiricism, Semantics, and Ontology', *Revue Internationale de Philosophie*, 4(11): 20–40. Reprinted in Carnap 1956, pp. 205–21.

Carnap, R. 1956. *Meaning and Necessity: A Study in Semantics and Modal Logic*, 2nd ed., Chicago: University of Chicago Press.

Carnap, R. 1963. 'Intellectual Autobiography', in P. A. Schilpp (ed.), *The Philosophy of Rudolf Carnap*, La Salle, Illinois, Open Court, pp. 1–84.

Carus, A. W. 2007. *Carnap and Twentieth-Century Thought: Explication as Enlightenment*, Cambridge: Cambridge University Press.

Cohnitz, D., and Rossberg, M. 2006. *Nelson Goodman*, Chesham: Acumen. Reprinted in 2014, Chesham: Routledge.

Cox, D. 2003. 'Goodman and Putnam on the Making of Worlds', *Erkenntnis*, 58: 33–46.

Daly, C. 2005. 'So Where's the Explanation?', in H. Beebee and J. Dodd (eds.), *Truthmakers: The Contemporary Debate*, Oxford: Clarendon Press, pp. 17–31.

Dasgupta, S. 2018. 'Realism and the Absence of Value', *The Philosophical Review*, 127(3): 279–322.

David, M. 2018. 'The Correspondence Theory of Truth', in M. Glanzberg (ed.), *The Oxford Handbook of Truth*, New York: Oxford University Press, pp. -238–58.

Davidson, J. D. 1991. 'Appearances, Antirealism, and Aristotle', *Philosophical Studies*, 63(2): 147–66.

Devitt, M. 1983. 'Realism and the Renegade Putnam: A Critical Study of *Meaning and the Moral Sciences*', *Noûs*, 17(2): 291–301.

Devitt, M. 1991. *Realism and Truth*, 2nd ed., Princeton: Princeton University Press.

Devitt, M. 2008. 'Realism/Anti-Realism', in S. Psillos and M. Curd (eds.), *Routledge Companion to the Philosophy of Science*, Oxford: Routledge, pp. 224–35.

Devitt, M. 2010. *Putting Metaphysics First: Essays on Metaphysics and Epistemology*, Oxford: Oxford University Press.

deVries, W. A. 2009. 'Getting beyond Idealism', in W. A. deVries (ed.), *Empiricism, Perceptual Knowledge, Normativity, and Realism: Essays on Wilfrid Sellars*, Oxford: Oxford University Press, pp. 211–45.

Dorr, C. 2005. 'What We Disagree About When We Disagree About Ontology', in M. Kalderon (ed.), *Fictionalism in Metaphysics*, Oxford: Oxford University Press, pp. 234–86.

Dudau, R. 2002. *The Realism/Anti-Realism Debate in the Philosophy of Science*, Berlin: Logos.

Dummett, M. 1963. 'The Philosophical Significance of Gödel's Theorem', in *Truth and Other Enigmas*, Cambridge, MA: Harvard University Press, pp. 186–214.

Dummett, M. 1978. *Truth and Other Enigmas*, Cambridge, MA: Harvard University Press.

Dummett, M. 1981. *Frege: Philosophy of Language*, 2nd ed., Cambridge, MA: Harvard University Press.

Dummett, M. 1982. 'Realism', *Synthese*, 52: 55–112.

Dummett, M. 1993. *The Logical Basis of Metaphysics*, Cambridge, MA: Harvard University Press.

Dummett, M. 2005. 'The Justificationist's Response to a Realist', *Mind*, 114(455): 671–88.

Edgington, D. 1981. 'Meaning, Bivalence and Realism', *Proceedings of the Aristotelian Society*, 81: 153–73.

Edmunds, D. 2020. *The Murder of Professor Schlick*, Princeton and Oxford: Princeton University Press.

Eklund, M. 2008. 'The Picture of Reality as an Amorphous Lump', in T. Sider, J. Hawthorne, and D. Zimmerman (eds.), *Contemporary Debates in Metaphysics*, Oxford: Blackwell, pp. 382–96.

Elgin, C. Z. 1995. 'Unnatural Science', *Journal of Philosophy*, 92(6): 289–302.

Field, H. 1988. 'Realism, Mathematics and Modality', *Philosophical Topics*, 16(1): 57–107.

Fine, G. 2003. 'Subjectivity, Ancient and Modern: The Cyrenaics, Sextus, and Descartes', in J. Miller and B. Inwood (eds.), *Hellenistic and Early Modern Philosophy*, Cambridge: Cambridge University Press, pp. 192–231.

Fine, K. 2001. 'The Question of Realism', *Philosopher's Imprint*, 1(2): 1–30.

Fine, K. 2006. 'Relatively Unrestricted Quantification', in A. Rayo and G. Uzquiano (eds.), *Absolute Generality*, Oxford: Oxford University Press, pp. 20–44.

Fletcher, J. 2016. 'Arguing About Realism Adjudicating the Putnam-Devitt Dispute', *European Journal of Analytic Philosophy*, 12(2): 39–54.

Florio, S. 2014. 'Unrestricted Quantification', *Philosophy Compass*, 9: 441–54.

Friedman, M., and Creath, R. (eds.). 2007. *The Cambridge Companion to Carnap*, Cambridge: Cambridge University Press.

Garfield, J. 2005. *The Fundamental Wisdom of the Middle Way. Translation and Commentary of Nāgārjuna's Mūlamadhyamakakārikā*, Oxford: Oxford University Press.

Goldberg, S. (ed.). 2015. *The Brain in a Vat*, Cambridge: Cambridge University Press.

Goldberg, S. n.d. 'Semantic Externalism', *Oxford Bibliographies Online*. http://doi.org/10.1093/OBO/9780195396577-0113.

Goldschmidt, T., and Pearce, K. L. 2017. *Idealism: New Essays in Metaphysics*, Oxford: Oxford University Press.

Goodman, N. 1955. *Fact, Fiction, and Forecast*, Cambridge, MA: Harvard University Press.

Goodman, N. 1978. *Ways of Worldmaking*, Indianapolis: Hackett.

Goodman, N., and Quine, W. V. O. 1947. 'Steps Toward a Constructive Nominalism', *Journal of Symbolic Logic*, 12: 105–22.

Greco, J. 2007. 'External World Skepticism', *Philosophy Compass*, 2: 625–49.

Green, K. 2001. *Dummett: Philosophy of Language*, Oxford: Blackwell.

Griffin, N. 1991. *Russell's Idealist Apprenticeship*, Oxford: Clarendon Press.

Guyer, P., and Horstmann, R.-P. 2021. 'Idealism', in E. N. Zalta (ed.), *The Stanford Encyclopedia of Philosophy*, Spring ed. https://plato.stanford.edu/entries/idealism/

Hamilton, S. 2001. *Indian Philosophy: A Very Short Introduction*, New York: Oxford University Press.

Hatfield, G. 2006. 'The Cartesian Circle', in S. Gaukroger (ed.), *Blackwell Companion to Descartes' Meditations*, Oxford: Blackwell, pp. 122–41.

Haukioja, J. 2020. 'Metaphysical Realism and Anti-Realism', in R. Bliss and J. T. M. Miller (eds.), *The Routledge Handbook of Metametaphysics*, Oxford and New York: Routledge, pp. 61–70.

Heil, J. 2003. *From an Ontological Point of View*, Oxford: Clarendon Press.

Heller, M. 2008. 'The Donkey Problem', *Philosophical Studies*, 140: 83–101.

Hellman, G. 1989. 'Never Say "Never!" On the Communication Problem between Intuitionism and Classicism', *Philosophical Topics*, 17(2): 47–67.

Hellman, G. 1992. 'The Boxer and His Fists: The Constructivist in the Arena of Quantum Physics', *Proceedings of the Aristotelian Society*, 66: 61–77.

Hirsch, E. 2002. 'Quantifier Variance and Realism', *Noûs*, 36(1): 51–73.

Hirsch, E. 2011. *Quantifier Variance and Realism: Essays in Meta-Ontology*, New York and Oxford: Oxford University Press.

Hirsch, E., and Warren, J. 2019. 'Quantifier Variance', in M. Kusch (ed.), *The Routledge Handbook of Philosophy of Relativism*, Oxford and New York: Routledge.

Horwich, P. 1990. *Truth*, Oxford: Blackwell.

Horwich, P. 1996. 'Realism and Truth', *Philosophical Perspective*, 10: 187–97.

Hylton, P. W. 1990. *Russell, Idealism, and the Emergence of Analytic Philosophy*, Oxford: Clarendon Press.

Irmak, N. 2013. 'The Privilege of the Physical and the Status of Ontological Debates', *Philosophical Studies*, 166: 1–18.

Ivanhoe, P. J. 2009. *Readings from the Lu-Wang School of Neo-Confucianism*, Hackett.

Janssen-Lauret, F. Forthcoming. 'Susan Stebbing's Metaphysics and the Status of Common-Sense Truths', in J. Peijnenburg and S. Verhaegh (eds.), *Women in the History of Analytic Philosophy*, Indianapolis, IN: Springer Nature.

Jenkins, C. S. 2005. 'Realism and Independence', *American Philosophical Quarterly*, 42(3): 199–211.

Jenkins, C. S. 2010. 'What Is Ontological Realism?', *Philosophy Compass*, 5(10): 880–90.

Kallestrup, J. 2011. *Semantic Externalism*, New York: Routledge.

Kant, I. 1997. *Kant: Prolegomena to Any Future Metaphysics: With Selections from the Critique of Pure Reason*, G. Hatfield (ed.), Cambridge: Cambridge University Press.

Khlentzos, D. 2021, 'Challenges to Metaphysical Realism', in E. N. Zalta (ed.), *The Stanford Encyclopedia of Philosophy,* https://plato.stanford.edu/archives/spr2021/entries/realism-sem-challenge.

King, R. 1995. *Early Advaita Vedānta and Buddhism: The Mahāyāna Context of the Gauḍapādīya-kārikā*, New York: State University of New York Press.

Kraut, R. 2020. 'Rudolf Carnap: Pragmatist and Expressivist About Ontology', in R. Bliss and J. T. M. Miller (eds.), *The Routledge Handbook of Metametaphysics*, Oxford and New York: Routledge, pp. 32–48.

Kuusela, O., and McGinn, M. (eds.). 2011. *The Oxford Handbook of Wittgenstein*, Oxford: Oxford University Press.

Langton, R. 1998. *Kantian Humility: Our Ignorance of Things in Themselves*, Oxford: Clarendon Press.

Lewis, D. K. 1983. 'New Work for a Theory of Universals', *Australasian Journal of Philosophy*, 61: 343–77.

Lewis, D. K. 1984. 'Putnam's Paradox', *Australasian Journal of Philosophy*, 62: 221–36.

Lewis, D. K. 2009. 'Ramseyan Humility', in D. Braddon-Mitchell and R. Nola (eds.), *Conceptual Analysis and Philosophical Naturalism*, Cambridge, MA: MIT Press, pp. 203–22.

Linnebo, O. 2018. 'Dummett on Indefinite Extensibility', *Philosophical Issues*, 28(1): 196–220.

Markosian, N. 2015. 'The Right Stuff', *Australasian Journal of Philosophy*, 93 (4): 665–87.

Marx, K., Engels, F., and Lenin, V. 1972. *On Historical Materialism*, Moscow: Progress.

McDaniel, K. 2017. *The Fragmentation of Being*, Oxford: Oxford University Press.

McGinn, M. 1997. *Routledge Philosophy Guidebook to Wittgenstein and the Philosophical Investigations*, London: Routledge.

McGrath, M. 2003. 'What the Deflationist May Say About Truthmaking', *Philosophy and Phenomenological Research*, 66(3): 666–88.

McNally, T. 2017. *Wittgenstein and the Philosophy of Language: The Legacy of the Philosophical Investigations*, Cambridge: Cambridge University Press.

McTaggart, J. M. E. 1921–1927. *The Nature of Existence*, 2 vols., Cambridge: Cambridge University Press.

Miller, A. 2019. 'Realism', in E. N. Zalta (ed.), *The Stanford Encyclopedia of Philosophy*, Winter ed. https://plato.stanford.edu/entries/realism/

Miller, J. T. M. 2014. *Realism, Truthmakers, and Language: A Study in Meta-Ontology and the Relationship between Language and Metaphysics*. Doctoral thesis, Durham University.

Miller, J. T. M. 2016. 'Can an Ontological Pluralist Really be a Realist?', *Metaphilosophy*, 47(3): 425–30.

Miller, J. T. M. 2021. 'What Counts as a "Good" Metaphysical Language?', in J. T. M. Miller (ed.), *The Language of Ontology*, Oxford: Oxford University Press, pp. 102–19.

Millikan, R. 1986. 'Metaphysical Anti-Realism?', *Mind*, 95: 417–31.

Moore, G. E. 1959. 'Certainty', in *Philosophical Papers*, London: George Allen & Unwin, pp. 226–51.

Moore, G. E. 1899. 'The Nature of Judgement', *Mind*, 8: 176–93.

Moore, G. E. 1903. 'The Refutation of Idealism', *Mind*, 12: 433–53.

Moore, G. E. 1925. 'A Defence of Common Sense', in J. Muirhead (ed.), *Contemporary British Philosophy*. London: George Allen and Unwin.

Moore, G. E. 1939. 'Proof of an External World', *Proceedings of the British Academy*, 25: 273–300.

Moore, G. E. 1959. *Philosophical Papers*, London: George Allen and Unwin.

Mueller, A., and Fine, A. 2005. 'Realism, Beyond Miracles', in Y. Ben-Menahem (ed.), *Hilary Putnam*, Cambridge: Cambridge University Press, pp. 83–124.

Ney, A. 2012. 'Neo-Positivist Metaphysics', *Philosophical Studies*, 160: 53–78.

O'Leary-Hawthorne, J., and Cortens, A. 1995. 'Towards Ontological Nihilism', *Philosophical Studies*, 79(2): 143–65.

Page, S. 2006. 'Mind-Independence Disambiguated: Separating the Meat from the Straw in the Realism/Anti-Realism Debate', *Ratio*, 19: 321–35.

Pagin, P. 1998. 'Bivalence: Meaning Theory vs Metaphysics', *Theoria*, 64(2–3): 157–86.

Parent, T. 2020. 'Ontological Commitment and Quantifiers', in R. Bliss and J. T. M. Miller (eds.), *The Routledge Handbook of Metametaphysics*, Oxford and New York: Routledge, pp. 85–99.

Pendlebury, M. 2010. 'Facts and Truth-Making', *Topoi*, 29(2): 137–45.

Pincock, C. 2009. 'Carnap's Logical Structure of the World', *Philosophy Compass*, 4(6): 951–61.

Price, H. 2009. 'Metaphysics after Carnap: The Ghost Who Walks?', in D. Chalmers, D. Manley, and R. Wasserman (eds.), *Metametaphysics: New Essays on the Foundations of Ontology*, Oxford: Oxford University Press, pp. 320–46.

Putnam, H. 1975. 'The Meaning of "Meaning"', *Minnesota Studies in the Philosophy of Science*, 7: 131–93.

Putnam, H. 1977. 'Realism and Reason', *Proceedings and Addresses of the American Philosophical Association*, 50(6): 483–98. Reprinted in Putnam 1978, pp. 123–38.

Putnam, H. 1978. *Meaning and the Moral Sciences*, Boston: Routledge and Kegan Paul.

Putnam, H. 1981. *Reason, Truth and History*, Cambridge: Cambridge University Press.

Putnam, H. 1987. *The Many Faces of Realism*, LaSalle: Open Court.

Putnam, H. 1992a. 'Irrealism and Deconstruction', in *Renewing Philosophy*, Cambridge, MA: Harvard University Press, pp. 108–33.

Putnam, H. 1992b. *Renewing Philosophy*, Cambridge, MA: Harvard University Press.

Putnam, H. 1999. *The Threefold Cord: Mind, Body, and World*, New York: Columbia University Press.

Putnam, H. 2004. *Ethics without Ontology*, Cambridge, MA: Harvard University Press.

Putnam, H. 2008. 'Wittgenstein and Realism', *International Journal of Philosophical Studies*, 16(1): 3–16.

Quine, W. V. O. 1948. 'On What There Is', *Review of Metaphysics*, 2: 21–38.

Rayo, A. 2020. 'Absolute Generality', in R. Bliss and J. T. M. Miller (eds.), *The Routledge Handbook of Metametaphysics*, Oxford and New York: Routledge, pp. 130–42.

Resnick, M. 1990. 'Immanent Truth', *Mind*, 99(395): 405–24.

Rickless, S. 2013. *Berkeley's Argument for Idealism*, Oxford: Oxford University Press.

Rorty, R. 2000. *Philosophy and Social Hope*, New York: Penguin.

Rorty, R. M. (ed.). 1992. *The Linguistic Turn*, Chicago and London: University of Chicago Press.

Royce, J. 1919. *Lectures on Modern Idealism*, New Haven: Yale University Press.

Russell, B. 1907. 'On Some Difficulties in the Theory of Transfinite Numbers and Order Types', *Proceedings of the London Mathematical Society*, 4: 29–53.

Russell, B. 1908. 'Mathematical Logic as Based on a Theory of Types', *American Journal of Mathematics*, 30: 222–62.

Russell, B. 1912. *The Problems of Philosophy*, Oxford: Oxford University Press.

Sandqvist, T. 2009. 'Classical Logic without Bivalence', *Analysis*, 69(2): 211–18.

Sidelle, A. 1992. 'Identity and the Identity-Like', *Philosophical Topics*, 20(1): 269–92.

Sider, T. 2011. *Writing the Book of the World*, Oxford: Oxford University Press.

Sider, T. 2020. *The Tools of Metaphysics and the Metaphysics of Science*, Oxford: Oxford University Press.

Siderits, M., and Katsura, S. 2013. *Nāgārjuna's Middle Way: The Mūlamadhyamakakārikā*, Boston: Wisdom.

Smart, J. J. C. 1982. 'Metaphysical Realism', *Analysis*, 42(1): 1–3.

Smart, J. J. C. 1986. 'Realism v. Idealism', *Philosophy*, 61(237): 295–312.

Smith, B., and Varzi, A. C. 2000. 'Fiat and Bona Fide Boundaries', *Philosophy and Phenomenological Research*, 60(2): 401–20.

Smith, D. C. 2002. 'The Case for Metaphysical Realism', *The Southern Journal of Philosophy*, 40: 411–19.

Sosa, E. 1999. 'Existential Relativity', *Midwest Studies in Philosophy*, 23: 132–43.

Spackman, J. 2014. 'Between Nihilism and Anti-Essentialism: A Conceptualist Interpretation of Nāgārjuna', *Philosophy East and West*, 61(1): 151–73.

Stebbing, L. S. 1929. 'Realism and Modern Physics', *Proceedings of the Aristotelian Society*, 9(Supplement): 146–61.

Stebbing, L. S. 1932–1933. 'The Method of Analysis in Metaphysics', *Proceedings of the Aristotelian Society*, 33: 65–94.

Stebbing, L. S. 1942. 'Moore's Influence', in P. Schilpp (ed.), *The Philosophy of G. E. Moore*, La Salle: Open Court, pp. 515–32.

Stern, D. G. 2004. *Wittgenstein's Philosophical Investigations: An Introduction*, Cambridge: Cambridge University Press.

Sud, R., and Manley, D. 2020. 'Quantifier Variance', in R. Bliss and J. T. M. Miller (eds.), *The Routledge Handbook of Metametaphysics*, Oxford and New York: Routledge, pp. 100–17.

Tahko, T. 2012. 'Boundaries in Reality', *Ratio*, 25: 405–24.

Taylor, B. 1993. 'On Natural Properties in Metaphysics', *Mind*, 102(405): 81–100.

Tennant, N. 1987. *Anti-Realism and Logic*, Oxford: Clarendon Press.

Thomasson, A. L. 2003. 'Realism and Human Kinds', *Philosophy and Phenomenological Research*, 67: 580–609.

Thomasson, A. L. 2009. 'Answerable and Unanswerable Questions', in D. J. Chalmers, D. Manley, and R. Wasserman (eds.), *Metametaphysics: New Essays on the Foundations of Ontology*, Oxford: Oxford University Press, pp. 444–71.

Putnam, H. 1980, 'How to be an Internal Realist and a Transcendental Idealist (at the Same Time)'. In R. Haller and W. Grassl, (eds.), *Language, Logic, and Philosophy* by Vol. 4. Proceedings of the International Wittgenstein Symposium. Vienna: Hölder-Pichler-Tempsky, pp. 100–8.

Thomasson, A. L. 2015. *Ontology Made Easy*, Oxford and New York: Oxford University Press.

Turner, J. 2010. 'Ontological Pluralism', *Journal of Philosophy*, 107(1): 5–34.

Turner, J. 2011. 'Ontological Nihilism', in K. Bennett and D. Zimmerman (eds.), *Oxford Studies in Metaphysics*, vol. 6, Oxford: Oxford University Press, pp. 1–54.

Uebel, T. E. 2018. 'Carnap's Transformation of Epistemology and the Development of His Metaphilosophy', *The Monist*, 101(4): 367–87.

Varzi, A. C. 2011. 'Boundaries, Conventions, and Realism', in J. K. Campbell, M. O'Rourke, and M. H. Slater (eds.), *Carving Nature at Its Joints: Natural Kinds in Metaphysics and Science*, Cambridge, MA: MIT Press, pp. 129–53.

Varzi, A. C. 2014. 'Realism in the Desert', in M. Dell'Utri, F. Bacchini, and S. Caputo (eds.), *Realism and Ontology without Myths*, Newcastle: Cambridge Scholars Press, pp. 16–31.

Walker, R. C. S. 2018. 'The Coherence Theory of Truth', in M. Glanzberg (ed.), *The Oxford Handbook of Truth*, New York: Oxford University Press, pp. 219–37.

Warren, J. 2017a. 'Quantifier Variance and Indefinite Extensibility', *Philosophical Review*, 126(1): 81–122.

Warren, J. 2017b. 'Epistemology versus Non-Causal Realism', *Synthese*, 194: 1643–62.

Westerhoff, J., 2016, 'On the nihilist interpretation of Madhyamaka', *Journal of Indian Philosophy*, 44:2, 337–376.

Westerhoff, J. 2018. 'Nāgārjuna', in E. N. Zalta (ed.), *The Stanford Encyclopedia of Philosophy*. https://plato.stanford.edu/entries/nagarjuna/

Westerhoff, J. 2021. 'An Argument for Ontological Nihilism', *Inquiry*. http://doi.org/10.1080/0020174X.2021.1934268.

Williamson, T. 2003. 'Everything', *Philosophical Perspectives*, 17(1): 415–65.

Williamson, T. 2016. 'Abductive Philosophy', *Philosophical Forum*, 47(3–4): 263–80.

Winkler, K. P. 1989. *Berkeley: An Interpretation*, New York: Oxford University Press.

Wittgenstein, L. 1953. *Philosophical Investigations*, G. E. M. Anscombe and R. Rhees (eds.), G. E. M. Anscombe (trans.), Oxford: Blackwell.

Wittgenstein, L. 1961. *Tractatus Logico-Philosophicus*, D. F. Pears and B. F. McGuinness (trans.), New York: Humanities Press.

Wolff, C. 1751. *Vernünftige Gedancken von Gott, der Welt, und der Seele des Menschen, auch allen Dingen überhaupt*, Neue Auflage hin und wieder vermehret, Halle: Renger.

Wright, C. 1992a. 'On Putnam's Proof that We are not Brains-in-a-Vat', *Proceedings of the Aristotelian Society*, 92(1): 67–94.

Wright, C. 1992b. *Truth and Objectivity*, Cambridge, MA: Harvard University Press.

Wright, C. 1993. *Realism, Meaning and Truth*, Oxford: Blackwell.

Wright, C., and Hale, B. 2017. 'Putnam's Model-Theoretic Argument against Metaphysical Realism', in C. Wright, B. Hale, and A. Miller (eds.), *A Companion to the Philosophy of Language*, Chichester: John Wiley, pp. 703–30.

Acknowledgements

My interest in metaphysics, and in the realism/anti-realism debate, was sparked during my time as a PhD student at Durham University, and some parts of this Element are based on work that was originally completed for that PhD. I am therefore indebted to the philosophical community at Durham, both while I was there as a student and since I have returned as a member of staff, for conversations, reading groups, conferences, and many other events, too numerous to list. Particular thanks to E. J. Lowe and Wolfram Hinzen, who were consistently generous and supportive supervisors, and the many members of the Metaphysics Reading Group who endured my insistence that we read work in the then newly (re-)emerging domain of metametaphysics.

My thanks also to Tuomas Tahko, the series editor for the Cambridge Elements in Metaphysics, and to two anonymous reviewers of Cambridge University Press. This Element was substantially improved by their advice and helpful comments throughout the reviewing process.

Over the past seven years, I have taught metaphysics (and metametaphysics) at Trinity College Dublin, Nottingham, and Durham, at a range of levels. Teaching these topics, whether to first years, graduate students or somewhere in between, has been incredibly helpful to force me to think hard about what I think and why, and to (try to) justify my realist instincts. Trying to persuade a group of sceptical students about the importance (or possibly the necessity) of metaphysics is something that is helpful to everyone who writes on these topics, and I am grateful to all those students for their excellent questions, insightful comments, and willingness to take (meta)metaphysical questions seriously.

Lastly, but most importantly, my thanks to Anna Bortolan, whose advice helped shape both the structure and contents of this Element. Writing a book while shielding in a global pandemic was not easy, and it is no understatement to say that this Element would not be what it is, nor likely be at all, without Anna's consistent and unfailing help and support.

Cambridge Elements ☰

Metaphysics

Tuomas E. Tahko
University of Bristol

Tuomas E. Tahko is Professor of Metaphysics of Science at the University of Bristol, United Kingdom. Tahko specialises in contemporary analytic metaphysics, with an emphasis on methodological and epistemic issues: 'meta-metaphysics'. He also works at the interface of metaphysics and philosophy of science: 'metaphysics of science'. Tahko is the author of *Unity of Science* (Cambridge University Press, 2021, *Elements in Philosophy of Science*), *An Introduction to Metametaphysics* (Cambridge University Press, 2015), and editor of *Contemporary Aristotelian Metaphysics* (Cambridge University Press, 2012).

About the Series
This highly accessible series of Elements provides brief but comprehensive introductions to the most central topics in metaphysics. Many of the Elements also go into considerable depth, so the series will appeal to both students and academics. Some Elements bridge the gaps between metaphysics, philosophy of science, and epistemology.

Cambridge Elements ☰

Metaphysics

Elements in the Series

Printed in the United States
by Baker & Taylor Publisher Services